T0159117

Concerto
for
Intelligence

Concerto
for
Intelligence

Alan Griswold

CONCERTO FOR INTELLIGENCE

iUniverse books may be ordered through booksellers or by contacting:

iUniverse
1663 Liberty Drive
Bloomington, IN 47403
www.iuniverse.com
1-800-Authors (1-800-288-4677)

ISBN: 978-1-5320-1515-1 (sc)
ISBN: 978-1-5320-1516-8 (e)

Print information available on the last page.

iUniverse rev. date: 01/16/2017

Contents

The Flynn Effect's Unseen Hand

The Flynn effect is now a well-known phenomenon, but it remains entirely unexplained. Defined as the consistently observed and population-wide generational increase in raw intelligence scores, the Flynn effect has drawn a multitude of candidates for its underlying cause—including heterosis, better nutrition, more abundant education, environmental complexity, and various combinations of the above—and yet no candidate offered so far has proven to be either scientifically or logically compelling. Thus the Flynn effect remains one of the great challenges of modern science, or as James Flynn (2007) has described it in his book *What is Intelligence?*, a series of puzzling paradoxes, paradoxes still in need of definitive resolution.

Often when a phenomenon proves to be this intractable, it is indicative of a misunderstanding of the problem domain itself. Human intelligence has garnered a great deal of study over the past century, including an ever-increasing focus on the neuronal aspects of the activity, leading these days to a nearly universal acceptance that intelligence is to be depicted entirely in terms of brain-based functioning alone. But the irony in this brain-based focus on human intelligence is that it has become the greatest obstacle in achieving an understanding of the Flynn effect. If human intelligence is indeed the equivalent of brain-based functioning, then a significant increase in human intelligence implies a correspondingly significant increase in brain-based ability, a conclusion that nearly everyone wants to accept (almost as a shibboleth), but a conclusion that nags nonetheless, because it stretches biological plausibility. It is the essential mismatch between the biological properties of a brain-based intelligence and the phenomenon of a rapid, inexorable and ubiquitous increase in human intelligence that suggests why progress on the Flynn effect has remained so conspicuously non-existent.

Therefore this essay will not approach the Flynn effect by offering yet another strained explanation for the presumed increase in human brain-based ability, a presumption this essay most adamantly denies. Instead, this essay will approach the Flynn effect by proposing a radical shift in the underlying problem domain, outlining an entirely different view of human intelligence itself, a view encompassing a much broader context than merely an exclusive focus on the human brain. This alternative view of human intelligence will be presented through the mechanisms of a simple model, a model that highlights two orthogonal aspects of human intelligence: 1. *environmental intelligence*, defined as the total amount of non-biological pattern, structure and form tangibly contained within the human environment, and 2. *neuronal intelligence*, defined as an individual's neural capacity to absorb and respond to *environmental intelligence*. It can be shown that it is *environmental intelligence* that serves as the sole driver of the Flynn effect, and that *neuronal intelligence* influences the Flynn effect not at all. It can also be shown that *environmental intelligence* is similar to but far more comprehensive than the concept known as environmental complexity. And finally, it can be demonstrated that it is this dual-aspect model of human intelligence that effectively resolves all the Flynn effect paradoxes enumerated by James Flynn himself.

Generational gains in raw intelligence scores were first noticed by several individuals—including Reed Tuddenham and Richard Lynn—but it was James Flynn in the 1980s who convincingly revealed the widespread nature of what has come to be known as the Flynn effect, uncovering from data set after data set a persistent rise in human intelligence that seemed to be manifesting everywhere, for everyone, and at all times. In the years since, the Flynn effect has attracted a good deal of study and ink—in large part because the phenomenon has continued to be regarded as surprising, and in large part because the phenomenon has continued to defy adequate explanation.

This unsettled state of affairs stands in stark contrast to several other areas of human intelligence research, including investigations into the source and impact of individual and group intelligence differences. Employing factor analysis, identical twin studies and many other tools of modern cognitive research, scientists have been able to demonstrate frequently and with great consistency that individual intelligence differences produce significant impact on such endeavors as academics and career, and that these individual differences are driven primarily by genetics and are almost certainly neurally based. These discoveries and achievements regarding individual and group intelligence differences, captured eloquently in the concept known as Spearman's *g*, stand as one of the great success stories of modern research and have led to a nearly unanimous consensus that intelligence is to be regarded exclusively as a brain-produced, genetically driven activity—in short, intelligence correlates directly to the neural effectiveness of the human brain.

The Flynn effect, however, throws a perplexing monkey wrench into this widely held view. To accept the conclusion that intelligence is exclusively a brain-produced activity, with the effectiveness of that activity determined in large degree by genetics, one must also anticipate that overall human intelligence will remain stable over time. This would be in accordance with all standard biological and evolutionary principles, because nowhere else in nature does one observe an animal species experiencing a rapid generational shift in its biological underpinnings or in its corresponding behavior. Humans have certainly experienced a massive shift in their *circumstances* over the last several millennia, a shift that has induced certain physical effects—the humans of today are for instance somewhat larger on average than they used to be—but this shift in circumstances should not mislead anyone into believing that humans have biologically transformed since their prehistoric days. The genetic signature of modern *Homo sapiens* versus ancient *Homo sapiens* remains fundamentally the same—as is to be expected of *any* animal species—and if one were to somehow get hold of a kidney for instance from a Cro-Magnon human, it would be utterly shocking to discover that that kidney was somehow different in its physical structure or biological functioning than the kidneys to be found in humans today. It is only with one particular biological organ, the human brain, that it has somehow become commonplace to assume that that organ is mutating dramatically from generation to generation. And indeed if the Flynn effect statistics from the twentieth century are to be believed, then the presumed widespread increase in brain-based ability from generation to generation has now entered the realm of biological miracle—or perhaps to put it a bit more soberly, has now entered the realm of biological magic.

This then is the essential conundrum faced by anyone claiming that human intelligence is exclusively, or even primarily, a brain-based activity.

Because either one further accepts that the physical structure and biological functioning of the human brain remains essentially the same today as it was a hundred thousand years ago—which becomes tantamount to a denial of the Flynn effect—or one further accepts that the physical structure and biological functioning of the human brain has been rapidly transforming from generation to generation—which becomes tantamount to a denial of every known tenet of biology and evolution.

A popular means of trying to escape this conundrum is to divorce the Flynn effect entirely from genetics and from evolution, and to look instead for an orthogonal influence on human intelligence that can adequately account for the generational gains in intelligence scores while not trampling upon any biological sensibilities. To put it in the words of James Flynn (1999), it seems as if some unseen hand is propelling scores upwards, and thus the solution to the Flynn effect must lie in the identification of that unseen hand. Furthermore, Richard Lewontin (1976) has already provided a straightforward analogy for how such a mechanism would work, invoking a sack of seed corn full of genetic variability divided randomly into two batches, one planted in soil containing adequate nitrates and the other planted in more barren ground. The individual differences *within* each batch would remain consistent and would still be attributable to genetic variation, but the overall difference *between* the two batches would be due solely to the pervasive impact of the nitrates—no tenet of biology or evolution would be violated, and yet the batch-to-batch improvement could still be readily explained. And thus the target of any Flynn effect investigation would seem to be ideally the identification of a real-world, intelligence-boosting equivalent to the role being played by the nitrates.

Nonetheless, such identification has proven to be frustratingly difficult. It has not been because of lack of attempts: advanced education, early education, more widespread education, better nutrition, scientific ethos, video games, television shows with increasingly complex plot lines, more graphical environments, greater exposure to intelligence tests—all these and many similar candidates have been offered as the influence that might be driving intellectual ability ever higher, and yet no candidate offered so far has proven to be even remotely convincing. One major reason for this failure is the utterly pervasive nature of the Flynn effect. Wherever and whenever intelligence scores have been available, the Flynn effect has been evident at every age, for all people, all places and all times, and thus any offered candidate as the influence driving the Flynn effect must of necessity be equally pervasive, a daunting barricade upon which every candidate falls. For instance the Flynn effect has been apparent even when and where education has not been advanced, early or widespread. The Flynn effect was conspicuous even before video games and television shows were a twinkle in anyone's eye. And the Flynn effect has been evident even when nutrition has been sporadic or poor, and where scientific ethos, graphical environments and intelligence tests have yet to gain much hold. The Flynn effect is literally omnipresent, which is something no offered candidate can manage to be, and the only feeble attempt to address this shortcoming has been to suggest that the influence driving the Flynn effect might consist of some type of *combination* of the above candidates, along with perhaps several others, a proposal that comes off sounding like less of a solution so much as a concession of defeat.

There is yet a further problem underlying these many attempts to identify an external cause of the Flynn effect, a problem that is less often contemplated but a problem that is ultimately more troubling. Although it is common to divorce the Flynn effect from genetics and from evolution, it is not at all common to divorce the Flynn effect from human physiology, in particular to divorce the Flynn effect from its direct association to the human brain. Each candidate offered as an influence for driving the Flynn effect—be it education, nutrition, or any of the others—each is offered with the tacit understanding that the candidate must be sparking an improvement in human brain-based ability, must be prompting an increase in neural effectiveness. Such an assumption seems only natural— indeed required—since it has become scientific dogma that intelligence is directly correlated with the neural effectiveness of the human brain. But that dogma allows a glossing over of any descriptive mechanism, leaving it entirely unexplained how better nutrition, more education, a video game, etc., could be transforming the workings of cerebral matter. Furthermore, it must be remembered that there *already* exists a presumed neural mechanism for producing intelligence ability, the one driving individual and group intelligence differences—that mechanism firmly linked to and justified by genetics and evolution. And now alongside this already well-established neural mechanism is theorized yet another, the newcomer much more vague about its justifying mechanics, but just as importantly, absolutely *enjoined* from any link to genetics and evolution (because remember, the whole motivation behind identifying an orthogonal influence for the Flynn effect was to avoid any trampling on biological sensibilities). Somehow these two distinct mechanisms, emanating from entirely different sources and reliant upon utterly independent means, one driving Spearman's g and the other driving the Flynn effect, are each supposed to co-exist within the same human skull, each spawning intelligence abilities in its own unique way, and each doing so without interfering in the slightest with the actions of the other. It could only be by way of the dogma, the dogma that insists human intelligence must be directly correlated with the neural effectiveness of the human brain, that scientists can so readily suppress their skepticism and find such easy plausibility in all this theorized neural jumble. Without the dogma, anyone hearing of this brain-based goulash of competing-yet-somehow-cooperating neural mechanisms would think they were being subjected to some kind of madness or joke, because there is nothing in any of this brain-based goulash that resembles either science or logic.

A reasonable alternative would be to drop the dogma altogether. Despite the widespread consensus, there is in fact no direct or conclusive evidence that human intelligence can be explained entirely as a brain-based activity. Although neuroimaging techniques become more powerful with each passing year, and although biometric tools become more sophisticated all the time, and although data and statistical analyses continue to multiply by leaps and bounds, there has yet to appear anything even close to a demonstrated, comprehensive and explanatory link between detailed neural activity and its corresponding intelligence behavior—the workings of the human lobes remain more mystery than established description. Furthermore, with every attempt to link the Flynn effect to genetics, evolution and physiology resulting ultimately in paradox, conundrum and contradiction, it would seem there is adequate motivation to consider the alternative, to consider an influence on human intelligence not associable to the human brain, and to divorce the Flynn effect not just from genetics and evolution, but to divorce it entirely from the human head.

Accordingly, this essay outlines a model of human intelligence that greatly expands the context of that conception, eschewing the notion that intelligence can be adequately described in terms of just brain-based functioning alone. The model describes human intelligence as the combination of two orthogonal components, each essential to intelligence but each acting in an entirely separate domain. One component is called *environmental intelligence* and is defined as the total amount of non-biological pattern, structure and form tangibly contained within the human environment. It is *environmental intelligence* that encompasses that aspect of human intelligence that is completely independent of the human brain, and it can be demonstrated that it is *environmental intelligence* that serves as the sole driver of the Flynn effect. The second component of human intelligence is called *neuronal intelligence* and is defined as an individual's neural capacity to absorb and respond to *environmental intelligence*. *Neuronal intelligence* is that aspect of human intelligence with which everyone is currently familiar, encompassing as it does all the brain-based elements of intellectual activity. But as its definition states, and quite unlike the *common* understanding of brain-based intelligence, *neuronal intelligence* does not capture all the essential features of human intelligence. Instead *neuronal intelligence* is meaningful only in conjunction with its more substantive counterpart, in conjunction with *environmental intelligence*, the stimulus to which *neuronal intelligence* is merely responsive.

The concept of *environmental intelligence* captures a phenomenon which not that long ago did not exist on this planet, but which these days has become so ubiquitous within the human world it is essentially taken for granted and overlooked. Humans once lived in an entirely natural setting and were once driven solely by biological need—just as is the case with wild animals today—and any pattern, structure or complexity to be found in that prehistoric world would have been provided by nature alone. But human circumstances clearly have changed, especially over the last fifty thousand years or so, and today humans find themselves thoroughly awash in all manner of artificial pattern, structure and complexity, and find themselves interacting continuously with a plethora of man-made constructs, far removed from any purely biological setting. Spoken words, jewelry, automobiles, music, baseball games, books, skyscrapers—to name just a few—all these newly arrived environmental artifacts embody an increasing cornucopia of pattern, symmetry, repetition, logic, structure and form, and these many environmental artifacts convey their embodied concepts not only to the extant human population, they preserve and accumulate those concepts for future generations as well.

To take just one seemingly simple example, a single library book—the symmetry of its external and internal construction, the linear and repetitive patterns running neatly across every page, the hierarchy of encodings beckoning throughout—in considering the form and complexity of a single library book, one quickly becomes overwhelmed by the sheer amount of structured material palpably contained within this seemingly simple example, and yet a single library book scarcely amounts to a single drop in what has become a palpably complex and ever-growing ocean. To do justice to the enormous impact that artifacts such as library books now have upon the human environment, one would need to multiply a book's structured material across the number of books contained throughout the world, and one would need to augment this total with the totals from all the other categories of artificial entity, and one would need further to boost this sum by the torrent of new constructions being inserted into the human environment each and every day. It is only after contemplating the tremendous volume of this elaborate calculation and it is only after weighing the staggering immensity of its ensuing result that one can begin to grasp both the conception and the definition of the term *environmental intelligence*, as the total amount of non-biological pattern, structure and form tangibly contained within the human environment.

That this increasing amount of non-biological pattern and structure would play a primary role in human intelligence should not come as a surprise. When observing and judging modern human activity, people frequently make note of the relative ability with which others absorb and respond to the environment's many artificial constructs—how well does one read a book, solve a math equation, program a machine, play an instrument, decode a map, navigate city blocks—and those who are seen as interacting more productively with these newfangled entities are the ones judged to be more intelligent. Plus this brand of judgment carries over too into that most direct assessment of intelligence, the IQ exam. An IQ exam's content is composed entirely out of non-biological features and challenges, an IQ exam's sole purpose is a reckoning of the test-taker's dexterity with artificial pattern, structure and form. Thus the content of an IQ exam serves as a proxy for the many newfound complexities of the human world, with a strong correlation between those who better master the proxy and those who better master the intricacies of modern living. And it is no coincidence that as the overall amount of pattern and structure continues to expand within the human environment, IQ exams of necessity must be modified to achieve similar transformation.

Artificial pattern and structure also form the *boundary* of intelligence, they constitute the observable extent of the intelligence domain. The fastest sprinter, the strongest weightlifter, the most prodigious progenitor—these feats are observed and measured by humans too but they are never categorized under the heading of intelligence. Intelligence has strict association with the non-biological, it is marked invariably by the presence of entities not to be found in the natural world. If for instance humans were to visit a distant planet and were to find there a variety of creatures engaged in the type of survival and procreative pursuit consistent with evolution, while finding little of anything else (much as Earth could have been described not that long ago), the visitors would say that although there is indeed life on this distant planet, there are no obvious signs of intelligence. If on the other hand, humans were to visit a planet where there was no biological life at all, and yet there could be seen everywhere an abundance of symmetrical, structured and patterned artifacts reminiscent of the types of constructions to be found on Earth today, the word *intelligence* would leap immediately to everyone's lips, and this without the presence of a single neural cell, without the presence of anything resembling a human brain. *Environmental intelligence* is the tangible emanation of intelligence, it is for all intents and purposes the physical location of intelligence itself. Without *environmental intelligence* there really could be no discussion of intelligence at all.

Because *environmental intelligence* is entirely open to observation, it is in theory measurable. This was hinted at in the discussion of the single library book, where quantification of the book's structured material was broadly contemplated, along with augmentation from the many other sources of structured material contained throughout the human world. But this example also illustrates that although measurement of *environmental intelligence* is theoretically possible, if one were to actually attempt such a feat it would inevitably degenerate into a pragmatic nightmare. How does one assign a distinct quantity to the pattern of a line of text? How does one supplement this amount by an assessment of the book's symmetry? And even assuming such non-trivial details could be resolved, there would still be the matter of the calculation quickly becoming unwieldy. *Environmental intelligence* is literally everywhere, it manifests at every layer of observation. *Environmental intelligence* has become so pervasive and has expanded to such hierarchical extreme that to assign any type of number to it at all would strain numberdom itself—not to mention human patience. The best that might be offered is an acknowledgement that while in the case of quantifying *environmental intelligence* the practical difficulties will almost always triumph over theoretical opportunity, it is still possible, using the broadest of strokes, to arrive at meaningful numeric conclusions. For instance, it can still be stated with confidence that *environmental intelligence* must have measured at absolute zero for quite some time, because it was not that long ago in Earth's history that there were no artificial features to be found in the environment at all. It can also be stated with confidence that *environmental intelligence* would have reached a more substantive level by say ten thousand years ago, when civilization was just beginning and humans were at the edge of recorded history. And it can finally be stated with confidence that whatever that ten-thousand-year-ago measure might have been, it would pale in comparison to any statistics that might be gathered today, where the complexity of a single city block would overwhelm any ancient total. The main quantitative conclusion to draw from *environmental intelligence* is that in recent human history it has been constantly and rapidly on the rise, and thus if one were to go in search of a candidate to match the Flynn effect's recent meteoric advance, one could do much worse than giving a nod towards the quickly changing dynamics of *environmental intelligence*.

As foreign as the concept of *environmental intelligence* might at first seem, the concept of *neuronal intelligence* by contrast is likely to be more familiar, encompassing as it does that aspect of intelligence to be associated with biology and the human brain. *Neuronal intelligence* scarcely needs much in the way of introduction, since it has been the subject now of more than a century's worth of scientific study, study that has produced many definitive and well-publicized results. *Neuronal intelligence* is measured primarily by relative scores on an IQ exam, *neuronal intelligence* is quantifiable through the notion of general intelligence or Spearman's *g*, *neuronal intelligence* is determined in large degree by human genetics, and *neuronal intelligence* is directly correlated to success in such endeavors as academics and career. With the advent of neuroimaging equipment and with the development of many classes of biometric tools, it has become increasingly feasible to observe various types of synaptic behavior and to pair this behavior with actual intelligence events, and although such experiments and analyses remain too crude for any type of detailed or descriptive understanding, the direct association of neural activity with human intelligence has become essentially undeniable. By every indication, *neuronal intelligence* is marked by an overall neural effectiveness, it is a product of the human neural system, it is a function of the human brain.

Nonetheless, the one thing this essay claims that *neuronal intelligence* is not, is a sufficient explanation for overall human intelligence. This insufficiency is stated directly in the given definition of *neuronal intelligence*, as an individual's neural capacity to absorb and respond to *environmental intelligence*. This definition, dependent upon another concept, remains entirely consistent with what is broadly known about neural systems, namely that they are mechanisms primarily of biological response, employed always in conjunction with external stimulus. Predator and prey, water and shelter, sexual target and foe—in the wild, whether by evolutionary instinct or through real-time species learning, neural systems are honed to be reactive to their surroundings, with the effectiveness of this reactivity often the determinant factor in matters of life and death. It is only in the supposedly exceptional case of human intelligence that a neural system is commonly assumed to have capacity that goes beyond responsiveness to the external world, it is only in the case of human intelligence that a neural system is assumed to be spontaneously capable of producing behavior heretofore unseen throughout the biological kingdom. This essay strongly rejects such assumptions, reserving for the human neural system only the role to which neural systems have been traditionally assigned, as agents solely of biological response, as reactors dependent upon external stimulus. In this way *neuronal intelligence* is not called upon to do anything biologically magical, it is not obligated to go beyond what is biologically common and known.

For those claiming however that human intelligence can be understood entirely in terms of brain-based functioning, the biologically magical is far less easy to avoid. The cerebral presence of intelligence itself is difficult enough to account for, given its unprecedented standing in evolutionary history. Add to this the observation that intelligence is significantly increasing with each generation, and the challenge only becomes that more daunting. Finally, consider that every explanation must be strictly confined to the workings inside the human skull, and it is little wonder that the pressure soon becomes irresistible to begin leaning towards the biologically fantastical. Modern explanations of human cerebral activity tend to invoke such notions as brain modules, brain pathways and brain regions, specialized areas of neural circuitry, each devoted to producing particular intelligence effects. One brain module for handling mathematical and logical reasoning, another brain pathway devoted to musical performance, finally an all-powerful brain region primed for linguistic activity. Every intelligence behavior, no matter how modern or how strange, must have its corresponding brain geographical counterpart, because in a system of strictly brain-based functioning it seems no other explanation can do. Unfortunately, these notions of brain module, brain pathway and brain region, despite their apparent necessity, remain entirely hypothetical at best, having never been demonstrated or described in anything resembling sufficient detail. And more disturbingly, one realizes that the Flynn effect imposes a particularly onerous requirement on all these brain-based components, demanding of each module, region and pathway that it undergo physical and functional improvement with each successive generation—an image quite at home in a science fiction movie, but an image that in the real world goes far beyond any known limits of biological and evolutionary plausibility.

The irony is, all these hypothetical brain-based components are entirely unnecessary. By reserving to *neuronal intelligence* only the traditional role of a neural system—as an agent strictly of biological response—and by assigning instead to *environmental intelligence* all the physical and expanding complexity that constitutes the hallmark trait of human intelligence, one can thereby untangle every biological and evolutionary concern. The logic of a math equation, the structure of a music performance, the pattern of a linguistic phrase—all these instances of human intelligence do indeed have a corresponding geographical counterpart, but that counterpart exists only in the external world, it does not exist inside the human head. To take just one seemingly simple example, a single library book—the symmetry of its external and internal construction, the linear and repetitive patterns running neatly across every page, the hierarchy of encodings beckoning throughout—nearly all the structural complexity to be associated with linguistic intelligence can be observed directly right there, can be taken in with little more than a glance, is laid out entirely right before one's very eyes. No neuroimaging equipment is required, no probing by the latest in biometric tools, no need to unlock deeper meanings within synaptic signatures. The structural complexity of human intelligence exists literally and palpably right there within the human environment, and to attempt to double this structural complexity by positing its neural equivalent within the human head would be to engage in nothing more than a redundant endeavor—dubious enough in and of itself, but made even more so by its fundamental conflict with the many tenets of biology and evolution.

Freed of such fantastical notions as enhanced brain modules, brain pathways and brain regions, and having to serve only as an agent of biological reaction (as it has always served), *neuronal intelligence* is under no obligation to undergo physical or biological change. Thus *neuronal intelligence* in humans today can be described as being essentially the same as it was in humans from tens of thousands of years ago, the only difference being that *neuronal intelligence* in humans today finds a great deal more *environmental intelligence* to which to respond. The rise in human intelligence is therefore not produced by alterations in biological brain-based abilities; the rise in human intelligence is produced instead by alterations in the non-biological human environment. It is *environmental intelligence*, itself under no biological or evolutionary constraint, that can be transformed at almost any conceivable pace. It is *environmental intelligence*, moribund for hundreds of millions of years on this planet, that has come to existence within the human world starting not that long ago, and has been rapidly accumulating ever since. And it is this increase in *environmental intelligence*—not any change or enhancement within the human brain—that can be identified as the sole driver of the Flynn effect.

With these understandings of *environmental intelligence* and *neuronal intelligence*, it is now possible to demonstrate how these two orthogonal influences in tandem can account for the salient characteristics of human intelligence, including the notion of a general intelligence captured by Spearman's *g*, and including the Flynn effect. Such demonstration can be accomplished through the means of a simple scenario, a scenario in which IQ exams are administered to representative groups of individuals at two distinct points in time, the times separated by several generations. This scenario will be in most respects unremarkable, since its IQ exam statistics will be stated in such a way as to reflect the type of IQ exam data that has been gathered consistently over the past many decades. But in one respect the scenario will be unique, because quite unlike what has been done in the real world, this scenario will give a transparent accounting of *environmental intelligence*.

To account for *environmental intelligence*, there are only two assumptions required. One, it must be assumed that the practical difficulties in measuring *environmental intelligence* can be theoretically overcome; and two, consistent with observation from recent human history, it is assumed that *environmental intelligence* will always increase between two generationally distinct points in time. These assumptions are actualized in the scenario by saying that humans have developed a scale for quantifying the amount of artificial pattern, structure and form contained within their physical environment, and that this scale is calibrated in something called environmental intelligence units, or EIUs. At Time 1—after measuring the patterns in many lines of text, after reckoning for the symmetry of countless buildings, after calculating the structural impact of thousands of streets and roads (and after assessing a good deal more)—humans have determined that the total amount of non-biological pattern, structure and form contained within this Time 1 environment measures in at 200 environmental intelligence units, or 200 EIUs. Furthermore, when this operation is repeated several generations later at Time 2—after accounting for how the means of communication have become more elaborate and widespread, after determining that the now larger architectural edifices have become more suffused with intricate supportive systems, after providing for how the modes of transportation have become much faster and greater ranging (and after assessing a good deal more)—humans have determined that the total amount of non-biological pattern, structure and form contained within this Time 2 environment now measures in at 400 EIUs. These numbers and units of measure are of course entirely arbitrary and serve only illustrative purpose, but it needs to be realized that the numbers and units are not of themselves essential to the demonstration. All that is required for the scenario is a means of quantification for *environmental intelligence*, along with an assurance that *environmental intelligence* will always increase over time.

The scenario begins at Time 1, where as has been stated *environmental intelligence* measures in at 200 EIUs. At Time 1, a standard battery of intelligence tests is administered to a broad sampling from the general population, and as is done with real-world intelligence exams, the raw scores are then normed and classified by rank. The essential characteristics of this process can be summarized by examining the results from just three individuals—call them A1, B1 and C1—individuals who represent respectively normed results that have been categorized as high intelligence, medium intelligence and low intelligence. The raw intelligence scores of these three individuals can be stated as the percentage of test questions each has answered correctly: for instance, before norming and ranking take place, it is noted that A1 has answered 80% of the test questions correctly, B1 has answered 70% correctly, and C1 60%. The results of all these Time 1 environmental and individual intelligence measures can be summarized by the following chart:

Time 1 (Environmental Intelligence: 200 EIUs)

	Raw Test Score	Normed Population Rank
A1	80%	High Intelligence
B1	70%	Medium Intelligence
C1	60%	Low Intelligence

From the normed results alone, standard research analysis regarding individual intelligence differences is performed in the usual manner, leading to the types of findings that have been categorized previously under the heading of *neuronal intelligence*. Employing factor analysis and incorporating an assortment of statistical and biological data gathered from the general population, scientists demonstrate with considerable confidence that, all other things being equal, A1 can expect greater success than his B1 and C1 peers in such areas as academics and career, and that the individual intelligence differences between A1, B1 and C1 can be attributed in large degree to their genetic background, and that these performance differences are largely quantifiable under the statistic of Spearman's *g* and reflect corresponding levels of overall neural effectiveness. As has been stated, this particular aspect of the scenario is entirely unremarkable, since it reflects the type of research and outcomes that have been consistently presented by intelligence researchers throughout the course of many years. Nonetheless, it should be noted that these findings are based entirely on *relative* rankings—the raw test scores do not come into play here, and there is no attempt to derive an *absolute* measure of intelligence. When it comes to determining the characteristics of *neuronal intelligence*, relative performance at a particular point in time is entirely sufficient to achieve nearly every meaningful result.

This does raise the question however of whether one can seek for an absolute measure of intelligence in addition to the universally employed relative rankings, and in this scenario, where *environmental intelligence* has been adequately accounted for, an absolute measure of intelligence is indeed viable. Recall that the raw intelligence scores of A1, B1 and C1 have been stated as the percentage of test questions each has successfully answered—80% for A1, 70% for B1, and 60% for C1—and this suggests that the raw intelligence scores of these three individuals could alternatively be stated as a percentage of *environmental intelligence* each has successfully mastered. This latter approach derives from the recognition that the content of an intelligence exam serves as a proxy for the artificial and structural complexity to be found in the human world, and thus serves as a proxy for *environmental intelligence*. If for instance the standard battery of intelligence tests being administered to this population could be described as a *perfect* proxy for *environmental intelligence*, then A1, by answering 80% of the test questions correctly, would be demonstrating a mastery of 80% of the *environmental intelligence* to be found in the everyday world. B1 and C1 would be respectively demonstrating a mastery of 70% and 60% of *environmental intelligence*. In reality, probably no intelligence exam can serve as a perfect proxy for *environmental intelligence*, and thus a factor of adjustment would be needed to account for any discrepancy, but in the interest of keeping the calculations simple, there is no harm in assuming that this particular battery of intelligence tests, in its totality, is a near perfect proxy for *environmental intelligence*—the assumption impacts only the calculated number, it does not disturb any of the resulting analysis.

Recognizing that the raw scores on an intelligence exam provide a direct link to *environmental intelligence*, and taking advantage of the fact that in this scenario *environmental intelligence* has been measured and quantified, it is now possible to provide an absolute intelligence score for each of the studied individuals. For A1, who has answered 80% of the test questions correctly—and with the battery of tests assumed to be a perfect proxy for *environmental intelligence*, and with the level of Time 1 *environmental intelligence* measured at 200 EIUs— A1's absolute intelligence score is calculated to be 160 EIUs, the result of multiplying 200 EIUs by 80%. For B1, the calculation produces an absolute intelligence score of 140 EIUs (200 EIUs x 70%), and for C1, the calculation results in an absolute intelligence score of 120 EIUs (200 EIUs x 60%). These results can be incorporated into the summarizing chart:

Time 1 (Environmental Intelligence: 200 EIUs)

	Raw Test Score	Normed Population Rank	Absolute Intelligence Score
A1	80%	High Intelligence	160 EIUs
B1	70%	Medium Intelligence	140 EIUs
C1	60%	Low Intelligence	120 EIUs

What might seem strange about this effort to derive an absolute intelligence score is that at Time 1 it will make no difference whatsoever. If researchers were to make use of the absolute intelligence scores instead of the relative rankings, they would still arrive at all the same conclusions. Intelligence differences would still be attributable to genetic causes, there would still be the same correlative success with academics and career, and Spearman's *g* would still emerge. Thus it might seem that the calculation of an absolute intelligence score is of no scientific value at all, is little more than a waste of time and effort. But such a conclusion would be premature. An absolute intelligence score does indeed contain valuable information— perhaps the most valuable information of all—but this information does not become apparent until the entire operation is repeated, is repeated several generations later at Time 2.

At Time 2, where *environmental intelligence* has been measured at 400 EIUs, the standard battery of intelligence tests is again administered to a broad sampling from the general population, and as was done at Time 1, the raw scores are then normed and classified by rank. A1, B1 and C1 are of course no longer part of the extant population, but the Time 2 results suggest that they have been equivalently replaced by three similar individuals—call them A2, B2 and C2—individuals who continue to represent normed results that have been categorized as high intelligence, medium intelligence and low intelligence. Indeed so similar are these three individuals to their Time 1 counterparts that their raw intelligence scores—that is, the percentage of test questions each has answered correctly—turn out to be exactly the same. A2 has answered 80% of the test questions correctly, B2 has answered 70% correctly, and C2 60%. The results of these Time 2 environmental and individual intelligence measures can be summarized by the following chart:

Time 2 (Environmental Intelligence: 400 EIUs)

	Raw Test Score	Normed Population Rank
A2	80%	High Intelligence
B2	70%	Medium Intelligence
C2	60%	Low Intelligence

Once again from the normed results alone, standard research analysis regarding individual intelligence differences is performed in the usual manner, leading once again to the types of findings that can be categorized under the heading of *neuronal intelligence*. And quite notably, all the Time 2 conclusions remain exactly the same as the Time 1 conclusions. Scientists can still demonstrate with considerable confidence that, all other things being equal, A2 can expect greater success than his B2 and C2 peers in such areas as academics and career, and that the individual intelligence differences between A2, B2 and C2 can be attributed in large degree to their genetic background, and that these performance differences are largely quantifiable under the statistic of Spearman's *g* and reflect corresponding levels of overall neural effectiveness. The steadfast similarity in these findings from Time 1 to Time 2 strongly suggests that the characteristics classified under the heading of *neuronal intelligence* remain absolutely stable over time, just as might be expected of a phenomenon heavily steeped in physiology, genetics and evolution. And indeed if this is all there were to say about the Time 2 findings—if the findings could be limited to just the domain of *neuronal intelligence*—then the proponents of a brain-based intelligence would now find themselves very much at ease, for there is nothing in any of these Time 2 findings as stated so far that would be at odds with the tenets of biology and evolution.

However that is not all there is to say about the Time 2 findings. Because just as has been taking place in the real world, this scenario has experienced a significant anomaly.

The anomaly has first appeared within the battery of tests. The initial tests offered to the Time 2 population were the exact same tests administered to the Time 1 population, but as it has turned out, the Time 2 population has found nearly all the Time 1 questions to be exceptionally easy. Few individuals score below 70% on the original tests, and the large majority of the Time 2 population manages to score well above 85%. With the scores so bunched together and bumping against the performance ceiling, the original exams are no longer serviceable for determining relative rankings within the population. Scientists discover that they need to alter the exams—by beefing up the questions to contain greater complexity, by including topics recently introduced into the human world, and by suffusing the exams' content more generally with a greater amount of pattern, structure and form—and it is only after the scientists have made these alterations that the relative rankings similar to those evinced by the Time 1 population can begin to re-emerge. Thus the results presented above for the Time 2 population are not the results against the Time 1 battery of tests, they are instead the results against a much different battery of tests, tests that are in a very real and observable sense more challenging and more complex.

In one sense, the incorporation of this anomaly into the scenario is being driven by a desire to mimic happenings from the real world, where intelligence exams have been undergoing exactly the type of alteration as described above. But in a more compelling sense, the anomaly is being incorporated into the scenario because the very *conditions* of the scenario demand its inclusion. Recall that the contents of an intelligence exam serve as a proxy for *environmental intelligence*, and in this scenario *environmental intelligence* has significantly increased—doubled in fact—from Time 1 to Time 2. If the Time 1 battery of tests are serving as a perfect proxy for Time 1 *environmental intelligence*, then of necessity that same battery of tests cannot serve as an adequate proxy for Time 2 *environmental intelligence*. The beefing up of the questions' complexity, the addition of topics recently introduced into the human world, the inclusion of a greater amount of pattern, structure and form—all these changes are absolutely essential in order for the content of the Time 2 battery of tests to be a more accurate reflection of Time 2 *environmental intelligence*.

In many respects, this analysis reveals how the *content* of an intelligence exam serves as the linchpin for an understanding of human intelligence, and in particular for an understanding of the Flynn effect. It has been too common within the scientific literature to overlook the importance of the content of intelligence exams, and it has been too common within the scientific literature to treat the changing nature of intelligence exams as little more than a trivial side effect—somewhere between an annoyance and a curiosity—but these assessments are extremely short-sighted. The fact that intelligence exams must be regularly altered, and altered in a particular way, is perhaps the most important piece of information there is regarding the nature of human intelligence. It indicates that intelligence exams of necessity must reflect the structural nature of the external world, and it indicates that the structural nature of the external world is in a constant state of accumulation, and it indicates that this constant state of accumulation is playing a fundamental role in determining overall human intelligence. Consider what the content of an intelligence exam would have been like if presented in Mesopotamia around five thousand years ago. With language much simpler than it is today (and nearly always spoken), and with mathematics virtually non-existent, and with only a handful of abodes of just the simplest construction, the contents of an IQ exam from that era would of necessity been practically childlike compared to the exams offered today, and yet the majority of the Mesopotamian population would have found such "childlike" exams to be extremely challenging. By five hundred years ago, with language now more elaborate and transmitted in a greater variety of forms, and with basic arithmetic more well known and its impact more suffused throughout the surroundings, and with edifices reaching the height and breadth of Gothic cathedrals, the content of a sixteenth-century intelligence exam would have been far more complex than possible in ancient Mesopotamia; while on the other hand, with modes of transportation almost entirely non-mechanical, and with science and logic still in their infancy, and with electronic communication not even yet a dream, the content of a sixteenth-century intelligence exam would have been utterly simplistic compared to what is offered in exams today, and yet the sixteenth-century population would have still found those "simplistic" exams to be extremely challenging. The content of an intelligence exam must change over time because that content is a reflection of the structural complexity of the surrounding world, a structural complexity that in recent human history has been always increasing.

The impact of the anomaly becomes apparent also when comparing absolute intelligence scores. As was done at Time 1, it is now possible to calculate absolute intelligence scores for each of the Time 2 individuals, and for A2, who has answered 80% of the Time 2 questions correctly—and with the Time 2 battery of tests assumed to be a perfect proxy for Time 2 *environmental intelligence*, and with the level of Time 2 *environmental intelligence* measured at 400 EIUs—A2's absolute intelligence score is calculated to be 320 EIUs, the result of multiplying 400 EIUs by 80%. For B2, the calculation produces an absolute intelligence score of 280 EIUs

(400 EIUs x 70%), and for C2, the calculation results in an absolute intelligence score of 240 EIUs (400 EIUs x 60%). In each case, these scores reflect a twofold increase over the absolute intelligence score of the equivalent Time 1 individual. In each case, these scores reflect a twofold increase in the amount of demonstrated intelligence. The results can be incorporated into the summarizing chart:

Time 2 (Environmental Intelligence: 400 EIUs)

	Raw Test Score	Normed Population Rank	Absolute Intelligence Score
A2	80%	High Intelligence	320 EIUs
B2	70%	Medium Intelligence	280 EIUs
C2	60%	Low Intelligence	240 EIUs

A comparison of the above chart with its Time 1 equivalent reveals that variation in human intelligence needs to be understood across two separate and independent domains. For the characteristics associated with *neuronal intelligence*—characteristics that find their basis in physiology, genetics and evolution—there is variation across the population but there is stability over time. For the characteristics associated with *environmental intelligence*—characteristics that find their literal home within the human surroundings—there is stability across the population but there is variation over time.

If the statement is offered suggesting that the Time 2 individuals are more intelligent than their Time 1 ancestors, it can be seen that there is inherent ambiguity in that statement. In the context of *neuronal intelligence*, referring to human neural capacity, the Time 2 individuals on average evince exactly the same level of neural capacity as do their Time 1 ancestors. But in the context of *environmental intelligence*, referring to the types and amounts of intelligence actually demonstrated, the Time 2 individuals, in a very real and observable sense, demonstrate a significantly greater level of intelligence than do their Time 1 counterparts. These assessments are not contradictory. They simply reveal the dual-aspect nature of human intelligence. Human intelligence is composed fundamentally of both *neuronal intelligence* and *environmental intelligence*, and it is only after these two orthogonal influences are both taken fully into account that the characteristics of human intelligence can be fully understood, including the notion of a general intelligence captured by Spearman's *g*, and including the Flynn effect.

In his book *What is Intelligence?*, James Flynn outlines four paradoxes he associates with the Flynn effect—the intelligence paradox, the mental retardation paradox, the identical twins paradox, and the factor analysis paradox. But seen in the light of both *neuronal intelligence* and *environmental intelligence*, it becomes apparent that what Flynn is describing are not really paradoxes at all. Instead, what Flynn is describing are unjustified conflations of *neuronal intelligence* and *environmental intelligence*, conflations motivated by the scientific dogma that everything associated with human intelligence must be invariably linked to the human brain.

Two of the paradoxes—the ones labeled *the intelligence paradox* and *the mental retardation paradox*—state the apparent incongruity that if the Flynn effect were literally true, then humans from one generation would be too implausibly dumb or too implausibly smart compared to humans from a different generation. In Flynn's words:

> "If huge IQ gains are intelligence gains, why are we not struck by the extraordinary subtlety of our children's conversation? Why do we not have to make allowances for the limitations of our parents? A difference of some 18 points in Full Scale IQ over two generations ought to be highly visible.
>
> "If we project IQ gains back to 1900, the average IQ scored against current norms was somewhere between 50 and 70. If IQ gains are in any sense real, we are driven to the absurd conclusion that a majority of our ancestors were mentally retarded."

The resolution to these two paradoxes is to recognize that Flynn is confusing the two different components of human intelligence; he is confusing *environmental intelligence* with *neuronal intelligence*. In particular, he is using the changed levels in one component (*environmental intelligence*) to infer a corresponding change in the other component (*neuronal intelligence*). That inference is entirely unwarranted.

Consider the individual named A1 in the scenario. At Time 1, A1 is assessed to be highly intelligent. He demonstrates an above-average ability to absorb and respond to *environmental intelligence* by correctly answering 80% of the test questions presented to him, and as A1 adroitly navigates through his Time 1 world, it can be anticipated he will experience relatively greater achievement in such areas as academics and career compared for instance to his B1 and C1 peers. But when A1's absolute (raw) intelligence score of 160 EIUs is compared to the population of Time 2, A1 suddenly appears to be much less smart. 160 EIUs scores well below the 240 EIUs of C2, a person assessed to be of low intelligence at Time 2. If 240 EIUs is considered to be of low intelligence at Time 2, then A1's score of 160 EIUs seems to mark him as a borderline imbecile.

So which is it? Is A1 highly intelligent or is he an imbecile? This paradox is resolved by recognizing that A1's *neuronal intelligence* is not subject to change. A1's absolute intelligence score of 160 EIUs has as much to do with the time period during which it was registered as it has to do with A1's biological capacity. If A1 could be magically transported forward in time and raised in the Time 2 world, he would absorb and respond to about 80% of the Time 2 *environmental intelligence* and would score correspondingly on a Time 2 intelligence exam, making it clear once again that he is a highly intelligent individual. A1's apparently low score of 160 EIUs has nothing to do with A1's neural capacity; it has everything to do with the change in *environmental intelligence* from Time 1 to Time 2.

This works exactly the same way going backwards in time. Consider C2, who is assessed at Time 2 to be of low intelligence. But when C2's absolute (raw) intelligence score of 240 EIUs is compared to the Time 1 population, where a score of 160 EIUs is considered to be highly intelligent, C2 suddenly comes across as a Mensa candidate, and one wonders if C2 simply had the misfortune of being born too late.

So which is it? Is C2 of low intelligence or is he a Mensa candidate? Once again, the resolution is to recognize that C2's *neuronal intelligence* is not subject to change. If C2 could be magically transported back in time and raised in the Time 1 world, he would absorb only about 60% of the Time 1 *environmental intelligence* and would score relatively poorly on the Time 1 intelligence exam. The timing of one's birth does not alter one's personal intellectual ability.

In addition to these examples from the scenario, Flynn provides a real-world occurrence that brings out both the paradox and its resolution in the most enlightening of ways. After noting that the average raw intelligence score from around the year 1900 would translate to an IQ of about 50 to 70 on today's scale, Flynn raises the specter of the following tableau:

> "Jensen relates an interview with a young man with a Wechsler IQ of 75. Despite the fact that he attended baseball games frequently, he was vague about the rules, did not know how many players were on a team, could not name the teams his home team played, and could not name any of the most famous players.
>
> "When Americans attended baseball games a century ago, were almost half of them too dull to follow the game or use a scorecard? My father who was born in 1885 taught me to keep score and spoke as if this was something virtually everyone did when he was a boy. How did Englishmen play cricket in 1900? Taking their mean IQ at face value, most of them would need a minder to position them in the field, tell them when to bat, and tell them when the innings was over."

This is a quintessential example of mistaking a change in raw intelligence scores as the evidence of a change in *neuronal intelligence*, when in fact it is only the evidence of a change in *environmental intelligence*. Think about incorporating questions dealing with baseball rules into an intelligence exam. If such questions had appeared on an exam in say the year 1800, no one at all, including the smartest people who then lived, would have been able to answer such questions correctly (other than by random luck). By contrast, if such questions were to appear on today's intelligence exams, many individuals, including those of low-to-average intelligence, would be able to answer such questions correctly—baseball and its rules have become an established part of the human environment, their widespread presence and influence are now thoroughly encountered and absorbed by a large percentage of the population. As Flynn indicates, it would be only those with an IQ of around 75 or under who would have limited potential to answer such questions correctly.

So does any of this mean that the smartest people from the year 1800 had the same intellectual capacity as Jensen's young man? It of course does not mean that at all.

The critical moment in time would have been around the year 1900. If questions regarding baseball rules had appeared on intelligence exams at that time, the results would have been decidedly mixed. Some people would have been able to answer such questions correctly, but many others would not, including those of otherwise average-to-high intelligence, and this only because baseball had not yet become widely entrenched within the human environment (it was just then catching on). But after the exam was finished, if one of those baseball-ignorant, question-misanswering persons of average-to-high intelligence had been taken to the ballpark, bought a ticket, sat with in the grandstands, explained the rules, given a scorecard and a pencil, a perfectly capable set of behaviors would have swiftly emerged. After all, this is a person of average-to-high intelligence, this person can absorb and respond to baseball rules just fine, they will give this person not the slightest bit of trouble. And around the year 1900, this scene would have actually been taking place, again and again and again—an example of additional pattern, structure and form being inserted into the human environment, an example of an increasing amount of *environmental intelligence*. And should a scientist of that era have found the need to add something new to the standard battery of intelligence tests—something that would have helped make the questions more challenging and more discerning than the now too easy nineteenth-century exams—the inclusion of a few baseball-inspired problems might have neatly done the trick.

The widespread increase in raw intelligence scores from 1900 to 2000 has everything to do with the increasing amount of *environmental intelligence* (including the addition of baseball rules). It has nothing to do with individual neural abilities. It has nothing to do with *neuronal intelligence*.

Another Flynn paradox is the one called *the identical twins paradox*. Flynn's words again:

> "There is no doubt that twins separated at birth, and raised apart, have very similar IQs, presumably because of their identical genes. Indeed a wide range of studies show that genes dominate individual differences in IQ and that environment is feeble. And yet, IQ gains are so great as to signal the existence of environmental factors of enormous potency. How can environment be both so feeble and so potent?"

The short answer to Flynn's question is to say that environment, despite Flynn's doubts, is indeed both feeble and potent. It is feeble when considering individual and group intelligence differences that manifest across the population—the domain in which neurology and genetics hold sway. And environment is potent when considering intelligence differences that manifest across time—the domain in which neurology and genetics possess no influence at all. But although this short answer does manage to resolve the paradox precisely, it does not address what is actually at issue here—namely why does Flynn think this is a paradox.

There are several different analogies one might use to illustrate this essay's dual-component model of human intelligence with its orthogonal influences of *neuronal intelligence* and *environmental intelligence*. For instance, Lewontin's example of the batches of seed corn would do quite well. Also, one might think of the heights of ships floating in a harbor, heights that differ from one another because of each ship's inherent characteristics (individual differences at a particular moment in time) and yet that can also deviate *in toto* because of the rising and falling tide (an environmental influence across time). Flynn of course would not find either Lewontin's example of the seed corn or the example of the rising and falling ships to be paradoxical, and yet when that exact same mechanism is suggested for human intelligence he seems to find himself in total disbelief. The question is why.

Flynn's disbelief arises from an ingrained assumption common to nearly every intelligence researcher—each has become entirely convinced that every intelligence characteristic, every intelligence difference, must be ultimately portrayed as a *neural* characteristic, as a *neural* difference. In other words, if an influence has no tangible impact upon the human brain, then it cannot be an influence associated with human intelligence. Thus when Flynn considers environmental forces, which he can see full well have the perfect potential for explaining the Flynn effect, he stops short when he does not see how those environmental forces can cause the supposedly requisite change in human genetics or human neurology. This would be the equivalent of Flynn stopping short because he does not see how the nitrates in the soil can impact the seed corn's genetic structure, or stopping short because he does not see how the water level in the harbor can alter the ships' physical characteristics. Flynn does not make this mistake when considering the seed corn or the ships in the harbor because he understands that the actions of the nitrates are *orthogonal* to the seed corn's genetics, and he understands that the water level in the harbor is *independent* of each ship's physical characteristics. But in the field of human intelligence, where it has become dogma that every influence must ultimately deliver its impact within the folds of the human brain, Flynn cannot countenance this kind of orthogonality, cannot countenance any degree of independence.

And yet that countenance is all that is required. When one drops the dogma that everything associated with human intelligence must be invariably linked to the human brain, and when one correspondingly accepts the orthogonal relationship between *neuronal intelligence* and *environmental intelligence*, then the supposed conflict between biological and environmental forces quickly loses its bite, and the dilemma of the identical twins paradox swiftly disappears.

The remaining Flynn paradox is *the factor analysis paradox*:

> "How can intelligence be both one and many at the same time or how can IQ gains be so contemptuous of g loadings? How can people get more intelligent and have no larger vocabularies, no larger stores of general information, no greater ability to solve arithmetical problems?"

The first question in Flynn's statement can be answered in the most straightforward of ways: IQ gains across time can be so contemptuous of *g* loadings because IQ gains across time have absolutely nothing to do with *neuronal intelligence*, and therefore have absolutely nothing to do with Spearman's *g*. In fact, *contemptuous* may not be the right word for it; *utter indifference* would more precisely capture the relationship.

The second question in Flynn's statement—why are intelligence gains differential across various aspects of intelligence—that question is more intriguing and allows for a deeper investigation into the characteristics of *environmental intelligence*. In this essay so far, and with the intent of keeping the discussion basic, *environmental intelligence* has always been taken as a whole, with an emphasis on the principle that taken as a whole, *environmental intelligence* is always increasing over time. But when *environmental intelligence* is examined under its various aspects, it can be seen that within these aspects varying rates of increase can frequently occur. Flynn's example of arithmetic provides a case in point. By the time the first intelligence exams were being administered in the early 1900s, arithmetic was already a well-established and deeply plumbed subject, and its impact had already become widely infused into the human surroundings. Thus there would be only minimal gains in arithmetical knowledge and influence throughout the twentieth century, a fact reflected in the corresponding minimal gains in arithmetic-based intelligence scores. But this would not have always been the case. As was noted previously, if there had been intelligence exams in Mesopotamia around five thousand years ago, arithmetic would have scarcely made an appearance, since much of the subject was still unknown; and yet at some point in human history, arithmetic must have become more deeply and widely established, infiltrating both the environment and the population, and if intelligence exams had been available during that period, the corresponding rapid increase in arithmetical ability would have been quite conspicuous. During this past century, while changes in vocabulary, general information and arithmetic have remained relatively quiet, rapid advances in electronic communication and modes of transportation have been producing tremendous amounts of embodied graphical structure and logical formulation into the human environment, leading to corresponding surges in associated intelligence scores. Thus the overall increase in *environmental intelligence* remains inexorable, even if the pace across its various components remains not entirely uniform.

Plus Flynn's concern regarding the differing rates of intelligence gain seems to be mostly a *neural* concern—otherwise why attempt to tie it to Spearman's *g*. But as noted already, intelligence gains are not produced by changing neural abilities. Intelligence gains require something that is far more malleable, something that can indeed be altered at differing rates and in differing ways. Intelligence gains require something with the characteristics of *environmental intelligence*.

Of the many theories that have been proposed to explain the Flynn effect, the one most similar to the model being presented here is the notion that gains are being driven by an increased exposure to environmental and social complexity. Schooler (1998) and Greenfield (1998) provide introductions to the subject, and in general it is not uncommon to hear it suggested that everything from urbanization to the widespread use of such items as puzzles, graphics and games must have something to do with the increased levels of human intelligence. These suggestions are certainly on the right track, but when they are examined in detail it can be seen that in at least two crucial respects their ability to account for the Flynn effect remains ultimately inadequate.

The first difficulty with these proposed notions of increased exposure to environmental and social complexity is that their proponents tend to focus on certain *things* within the environment, and miss the impact of the environment as a whole. For instance, two commonly touted examples of the type of environmental complexity that can lead to increased human intelligence are the widespread use of video games and the growing complexity and multivariate plot lines in television shows and movies. Others will highlight the expanded task demands that have come with increased urbanization, and some might point to the denser presence of visual symbols and graphical puzzles within everyday life. But no matter what thing or set of things is being proposed, it quickly becomes clear that these items by themselves cannot account for the ubiquitous and inexorable reach of the Flynn effect. The Flynn effect was working its magic long before there even were video games and television sets, and the Flynn effect remains prominent in locations where visual symbols and graphical puzzles have yet to take much hold, and the Flynn effect can even be noticed in rural as well as urban communities. Of course other instances of environmental and social complexity might be offered up instead, but inevitably each instance must fall victim to the shortcoming of having only limited spatial and temporal reach. The Flynn effect is a population-wide and time-persistent phenomenon, and so any explanation must have population-wide and time-persistent effect. A specific instance of environmental and social complexity will never fit that bill.

The second difficulty with the proposed notions of increased exposure to environmental and social complexity is that their proponents, like nearly everyone else, insist on tying these explanations to human neurology. Playing video games for instance might be characterized as expanding the capacity of working memory. Modern movie plots will be described as spawning a larger number of parallel connections within the logical neural circuitry. The increased task demands of urbanization are embraced as a type of ongoing cerebral training. It would seem that complexity by itself is rather useless, that its only real purpose is to prompt a restructuring within the neurons, to spark a rewiring between the ears. Such ideas run amok within modern science, but they lack parsimoniousness and plausibility, begging plasticity miracles within the confines of the human head.

This essay's description of *environmental intelligence*, while similar to the notions of increased exposure to environmental and social complexity, avoids the shortcomings of those notions by incorporating two significant improvements. First, *environmental intelligence* embraces a more comprehensive context than do the notions of environmental and social complexity, comprehensive enough to have population-wide and time-persistent impact, eschewing the focus on particular *things* within the human environment and incorporating instead nothing short of the total amount of non-biological pattern, structure and form tangibly contained within the human environment. Second, *environmental intelligence*, unlike the proposed notions of increased exposure to environmental and social complexity, severs the tie to human neurology, allowing *environmental intelligence* to accumulate without biological restriction, and without having to make resort to biological miracle.

One consequence that should be readily apparent from this essay's dual-component model of human intelligence is that the Flynn effect cannot be regarded as just a recent phenomenon. Tracking the historical increase in *environmental intelligence*, the Flynn effect will have begun near the time of the human great leap forward and will have been shadowing human existence ever since. And there is no reason to expect the Flynn effect will end anytime soon.

This essay has presented a new description of human intelligence, a description that retains the commonly accepted brain-based understandings, but a description that augments those understandings with an equally essential partner, with *environmental intelligence*, the total amount of non-biological pattern, structure and form tangibly contained within the human environment. This equally essential partner greatly expands the context of human intelligence and frees human intelligence from the confines of the human brain. *Environmental intelligence* places the structural complexity that is the hallmark trait of human intelligence into a far more observable domain, and it is the changing characteristic of that domain, the accumulating amount of artificial pattern, structure and form, that provides the most straightforward and non-paradoxical explanation of the Flynn effect. It is *environmental intelligence* that serves as the Flynn effect's unseen hand.

The Dickens-Flynn Model

The Dickens-Flynn model is an attempt by William Dickens and James Flynn (2001) to explain how environment and genes can interact to account both for environmentally driven increases in raw intelligence scores over time (the Flynn effect) and for genetically driven and stable individual intelligence differences within the human population (Spearman's g). On first glance there is much that appears promising about the Dickens-Flynn model, for it does directly address the observable tension between the Flynn effect and g, something that many explanations for the Flynn effect fail to do. And yet further inspection also reveals that the model is troubling in a rather conspicuous way—it sports the overall mechanics of a Rube Goldberg machine.

Perhaps the first thing to recognize about the Dickens-Flynn model is the degree to which leverage plays the key role. For instance in the authors' general outline of the model, small genetic advantages are described as being *amplified* through the means of a natural attraction to environmental surroundings that serve to *enhance* those advantages. Environmental influences on population-wide intelligence characteristics are said to be *boosted* through such factors as social multipliers and rolling triggers. And finally, genetic and environmental forces are depicted as mutually *propelling* each other by means of an hypothesized assortment of reciprocal feedback mechanisms. What might strike the reader is how stridently *mathematical* this model is, especially in its employment of such concepts as multipliers, triggers and feedback loops: instead of associating these terms to real-world examples or empirical descriptions, Dickens and Flynn more frequently cast them into the role of free variable, serving to balance out and drive their equations where required. Plus this tendency towards calculational necessity can be heard also in the authors' replies to the model's critics, where arguments against the plausibility of social multipliers and circular feedback mechanisms are frequently met by Dickens and Flynn with an appeal to such notions as simultaneous equations, estimated network effects and functional form.

None of this is to say that the Dickens-Flynn model is inherently wrong or essentially inconsistent. It remains perfectly conceivable that the model's many mechanisms and various factors can be fitted—with a little more mathematical tweaking perhaps—to the observable characteristics of human intelligence behavior. But even if this were so, parsing through such ideas as social multipliers, rolling triggers and reciprocal feedback mechanisms, one is left with the distinct impression that the Dickens-Flynn model can in no way be described as simple or straightforward, and this of course in stark contrast to the phenomenon which the model is intended to explain, a phenomenon which can be captured in very few words (human raw intelligence scores increase consistently and universally over time). A charitable way of depicting the Dickens-Flynn model would be to say that it is intricate and complex; a less charitable depiction would emphasize its propensity towards convolution.

Which raises a question: why would Dickens and Flynn insist on developing a model of such intricacy and complexity? Why did they not gravitate instead to something more direct, with fewer moving parts? Flynn (2007), ever the paragon of candor, provides a thorough and revealing answer in the pages of his book *What is Intelligence?* There Flynn notes that during the height of the intelligence race debates, Richard Lewontin (1976) had offered a compelling description for how an environmental influence could uniformly impact an entire population while still leaving undisturbed any of that population's genetically driven characteristics:

> "Lewontin tried to solve the paradox. He distinguished the role of genes within groups from the role of genes between groups. He imagined a sack of seedcorn with plenty of genetic variation randomly divided into two batches, each of which would therefore be equal for overall genetic quality. Batch A is grown in a uniform and optimal environment, so within that group all height differences at maturity are due to genetic variation; batch B is grown

in a uniform environment which lacks enough nitrates, so within that group all height differences are also genetic. However, the difference in average height between the two groups will, of course, be due entirely to the unequal quality of their two environments."

Although Lewontin's description proved mostly untenable within the context of the intelligence race debates, Flynn later recognized that it seemed to offer an ideal explanation for the Flynn effect:

"So now we seemed to have a solution. The present generation has some potent environmental advantage absent from the last generation that explains its higher average IQ. Let us call it Factor X. Factor X will simply not register in twin studies. After all, the two members of a twin pair are by definition of the same generation. Since Factor X was completely missing within the last generation, no one benefited from it at all and, therefore, it can hardly explain any IQ differences within the last generation. It will not dilute the dominance of genes. Since Factor X is completely uniform within the present generation, everyone benefits from it to the same degree and it cannot explain IQ differences within the present generation. Once again, the dominance of genes will be unchallenged. Therefore, twin studies could show that genes explain 100 percent of IQ differences within generations, and yet, environment might explain 100 percent of the average IQ difference between generations."

And yet as Flynn attempted to apply Lewontin's idea specifically to the Flynn effect, he quickly found himself frustrated:

"However, Lewontin offers us a poisoned apple. History has not experimented with the last two generations as we might experiment with plants in a laboratory. Consider the kind of factors that might explain massive IQ gains, such as better nutrition, more education, more liberal parenting, and the slow spread of the scientific ethos.

It is quite unreal to imagine any of these affecting two generations with uniformity. Certainly, everyone was not badly nourished in the last generation, everyone well nourished at present; everyone without secondary school in the last generation, everyone a graduate at present; everyone raised traditionally in the last generation, everyone raised liberally at present; everyone bereft of the scientific ethos in the last generation, everyone permeated with it at present. If the only solution to our paradox is to posit a Factor X or a collection of such, it seems even more baffling than before. We should shut this particular door as follows: a solution is plausible only if it does not posit a Factor X."

It is in this manner that Flynn begins to place a strange restriction around what he might deem to be an acceptable explanation for the Flynn effect: any explanation would have to carry all the desirable characteristics of a Factor X, but without actually *being* a Factor X. And it is into the space of this restriction that the Dickens-Flynn model comes to be. Flynn is quite forthcoming about what he perceives to be the model's most valuable characteristic:

"Best of all, our solution posits no Factor X."

It is from out of this historical context that one can get a better sense for why the Dickens-Flynn model must of necessity be so intricate and complex, and not simple and straightforward. It is as if Flynn has set forth the task of building a device designed to capture mice, and yet the device must in no way resemble a mousetrap. Therefore it is not all that surprising that the model's surveyors soon find themselves inundated with the equivalent of levers, pulleys, waterwheels, whistles and bells, and if the objection is made that in the end it is still just a mousetrap, then the model's architects can point to the enormous amounts of clever mathematical machinery and insist no one would mistake it for any such thing. And if the objection is raised that the mice are after all scurrying away, then the model's assemblers can suggest that perhaps a few more pieces of calculational duct tape and functional chicken wire should take care of the matter. Whether or not the many free parameters of the Dickens-Flynn model can ultimately be fitted to the characteristics of human intelligence is a matter difficult to judge, but that does not negate the readily made observation that the Dickens-Flynn model is quite frankly a massively entangled contraption.

Flynn's actual mistake is to have prematurely shut the door on a Factor X.

Flynn's reasoning is perfectly correct when he notes that not only is every iterated item on his Factor X list inadequate for explaining the Flynn effect, but that indeed *no* particular item or subset of items could conceivably possess the requisite power or ubiquitous reach to account for population-wide, generational increases in raw intelligence scores. But instead of giving up—instead of prematurely shutting the door—what Flynn needs to do at this point is to engage in some thinking outside the box, or perhaps to summon a phrase more germane to the problem at hand, what Flynn needs to do is to engage in some thinking outside the human skull.

In the essay *The Flynn Effect's Unseen Hand*, a model for human intelligence is presented in which the term *environmental intelligence* is defined as the total amount of non-biological pattern, structure and form tangibly contained within the human environment. *Environmental intelligence* serves as the all-encompassing, palpable location of human intelligence, and it has been the consistent increase in *environmental intelligence* over the course of human history that has served as the direct driver of the Flynn effect. It might not be entirely accurate to label *environmental intelligence* as a Factor X, since it is not really a factor, not a specific *thing*—instead *environmental intelligence* captures the impact of the structural surroundings *as a whole*. But nomenclature aside, *environmental intelligence* carries all the necessary characteristics of a Factor X. *Environmental intelligence* is ubiquitous. *Environmental intelligence* is constantly increasing. *Environmental intelligence* remains independent of the genetic influences driving individual intelligence differences.

The common objection that might be raised against a model of *environmental intelligence* is that it places the material location of intelligence firmly outside the human skull, firmly outside the human brain. But in exchange for jettisoning the widespread assumption that intelligence is a product strictly of human neurons—in exchange for accepting the total amount of non-biological pattern, structure and form as both the material substance of intelligence itself and as an ideal Factor X—what is regained thereby is a great deal of simplicity. Gone is the need for social multipliers. Gone is the need for triggers. Gone is the need for feedback loops. Indeed gone is the need for any type of genetic/environmental interaction at all, especially of the complex, intricate kind. What one regains by jettisoning the Dickens-Flynn model and by accepting instead a model of *environmental intelligence* is all the simplicity and straightforwardness that Lewontin must have originally had in mind.

It may no longer be fashionable in this era of modern statistical science, but simplicity and straightforwardness should still count for something. It is better to catch one's mice with a mousetrap.

Intelligence and the Flynn Effect, One More Time

Imagine an experiment that proceeds in the following fashion: there is a stage, and onto that stage researchers place boxes that are nondescript other than that each box has a small hole near the bottom from which water can freely drain. In the experiment, each box is left on the stage for precisely one hour, during which time the drained water is collected and measured.

The experiment consists of a broad sampling of such boxes, and it is discovered that there is a fair amount of variation in the results—some boxes produce more water, some produce less. The distribution of results comes out to be nearly normal, with a mean collection of 500 ml and a standard deviation of 100 ml. To provide some visualization for these results, the researchers summarize the experiment by placing three representative boxes onto the stage: a left box producing 400 ml per hour, one standard deviation below the mean; a middle box producing 500 ml per hour, exactly at the mean; and a right box producing 600 ml per hour, one standard deviation above the mean.

The study of these boxes is of importance to the researchers because the boxes serve useful purposes within the community. For instance food placed on top of a box does not spoil as quickly as it would otherwise. Furthermore, other experiments have shown that a box's usefulness is often proportional to the box's water production score, and although the correlations are not always exact they do tend to be statistically significant and emerge in all kinds of usefulness experiments. Based upon these strong correlations, the researchers define a box's usefulness to be the equivalent of its water production ability.

Curious about the variation in results and wanting to learn more about the underlying cause of the differing water production scores, the researchers conduct investigations that focus on the physical/generational characteristics of each box. Some of these characteristics, such as surface material and factory of origin, emerge as promising candidates, because variations in these characteristics correlate with variations in water production scores. Again, the correlations are not always exact but they do tend to be statistically significant and they do allow the researchers to predict water production scores to a reasonable degree of accuracy given any box's overall characteristics. These findings are strong enough to convince the researchers that a box's water production score and its physical/generational characteristics are tightly linked. The researchers begin to formulate theories about the nature of this linkage.

These experiments are repeated frequently, at least once each year, and the researchers notice that the overall results remain extremely consistent—same variation, same distribution, same correlations. All the prior years' findings are regularly verified, no theory gets overturned.

And yet over time, there does arise one nagging problem.

Despite the fact that almost every feature of the experiment remains exactly the same—same set up, same variation in results, same distribution, same usefulness, same correlations—despite all this remarkable consistency, the water production scores keep going up. They keep going up every year and they keep going up for all the boxes. The amount of increase each year is not overwhelming but it is large enough that it cannot be ignored. For instance, the collection containers that were used in the early years of the experiment eventually have to be replaced with larger containers to prevent spillage. After ten years of these experiments, when the researchers place the three representative boxes onto the stage to help visualize and summarize the results, the left box is now producing 480 ml of water per hour, the middle box is producing 600 ml, and the right box is producing 720 ml. The researchers recognize, with a good deal of consternation, that an average box now possesses the same water production ability as did a box one standard deviation above the mean from just ten years prior.

Many explanations for this phenomenon are proposed and investigated, beginning with a focus on the boxes themselves. Has there been a change in the surface material? The researchers discover that for a small number of boxes some slight alterations have indeed been introduced. Has there been a change in the construction process? Again the researchers find that one factory of origin has been mothballed and another has been remodeled, although the majority of the production facilities remain the same as before. The researchers look for still other clues, such as changes in size or weight, and although particular instances can be found, such changes are not pervasive. Indeed that becomes the telltale defect against all these explanations—each explanation accounts for only a small number of cases at best and appears entirely inadequate in the face of the widespread water production increase across boxes and across time.

The researchers then focus on the boxes' environment, thinking that this line of attack might uncover a more all-encompassing solution. For instance, a few of the storage facilities where the boxes are housed are now located at higher altitudes than they used to be. Other storage facilities have been reconstructed out of metal whereas they were formerly made out of wood. And some storage facilities have had a ventilation system installed. But here too, such circumstances account for only a limited number of cases, and furthermore, these environmental explanations suffer from a still more troubling defect, namely that no one can explain how an environmental change would translate into the necessary and corresponding change in the physical/generational characteristics of each box. Everyone agrees, as a consequence of the experiments conducted each year, that water production scores and the physical/generational characteristics of each box are tightly linked, so that any significant change in water production scores must of necessity be accompanied by significant changes in the boxes' characteristics. But how does an environmental change produce such an effect? How does a higher altitude, metallic surroundings or a ventilated facility produce the requisite alteration in surface material or point of origin? To many of the researchers, the connection seems implausible.

One researcher attempts to solve the dilemma by demonstrating how an environmental change and a physical/generational change can feed off each other with an amplifying effect. He uses terms such as *multiplier* and *feedback loop* and produces an impressive array of mathematics. "For instance a small change in surface material or production quality can generate a subtle difference in air flow around the corners of the box, which can alter the currents in the room, producing a multiplicative effect" he begins. "Then at the point of maximum air flow differential, a powerful feedback vibration is generated inside the box, and this vibration amplifies the rearrangement of surface material and boosts the air flow still further, which causes…"

Another researcher, noting the large number of explanations generated so far and the inability of each one to account for more than just a few cases, suggests that perhaps there is not just *one* explanation for the rising water production scores but rather the solution is to be found in a *combination* of explanations. This approach seems appealing to the frustrated researchers, although they have to agree it is not the kind of definitive answer they originally had in mind.

Then one day a visitor appears and has a suggestion for the researchers. "I don't know about you, but it seems to me that the weather keeps getting warmer all the time—I've been coming to your experiments for several years now, and every time I visit, it feels hotter to me than it did the last time. Then it occurred to me, that would make for an elegant explanation to your rising water production scores."

"How so?" ask the researchers.

"A general rise in temperature is the perfect match to what you're looking for, it has all the essential characteristics. For one, an increase in temperature would mirror the increase in water production scores. Two, an increase in temperature would be continuous over time—just as with the rise in scores. And three, a general increase in temperature would be ubiquitous, it would affect all the boxes nearly the same."

The researchers are not convinced.

"Here are the shortcomings in your explanation," they point out to the visitor. "In the first place, your explanation is not germane to the problem. We are investigating a box's usefulness, as measured by its water production score and contained in its physical/generational characteristics. It is hard to envision how ambient temperature can even be relevant to that discussion. But assuming it were somehow relevant, your explanation has an even bigger defect: you can't provide a plausible description for how a change in environmental temperature would alter the physical/generational characteristics of each box. Are you trying to suggest that a slight increase in temperature would somehow rearrange a box's surface material or reset a box's factory of origin? That would be ridiculous. If a change in ambient temperature were somehow the cause of a change in water production scores, then that change in temperature must also impact the physical/generational characteristics of each box, because those characteristics are the source of a box's water production ability."

The visitor ponders this statement for a moment, then gives a lengthy reply:

"I believe you're working under a mistaken assumption. Listen, I agree with you that variations in a box's physical/generational characteristics produce corresponding changes in a box's water production score—you have plenty of experimental evidence for that, and the results are strong and compelling. But your results are so strong and compelling that they seem to have convinced you that the inference is valid also in the other direction—that is, that every change in water production score is necessarily accompanied by a change in a box's physical/generational characteristics. But actually, you have no evidence that the inference is valid in that direction, all your evidence runs only the other way. Moreover, the increase in water production scores across time and across all the boxes suggests quite strongly that such an inference would be mistaken.

"Here is how I would describe the situation. We have three different quantities in play: a box's capacity to produce water, the water production score, and the ambient temperature. Let's let letters stand for each of these quantities:

C = a box's CAPACITY to produce water,
S = a box's water production SCORE, and
T = the ambient TEMPERATURE.

"A box's water production score (S) is the combination of the two other factors (C and T) working independently. This can be expressed in a simple relationship:

$$S = C \times T.$$

"That relationship fits your experimental results perfectly. At any given point in time, the ambient temperature (T) will be constant, so that when experiments are run at that time, all the variation in water production scores (S) will be the direct result of the differing physical/generational characteristics of each box, because those characteristics are what determine a box's relative capacity (C) to produce water.

"But *over* time it is the orthogonal effect that holds sway. Over time, it is C that remains constant. Your investigations have already told you this, because when you went looking for physical/generational changes across time that would help explain your results, you discovered that physical/generational changes across time are minimal at best, hardly worth the notice. But if C remains essentially constant, then all the increase in S over time is explained solely by an increase in T. The rising ambient temperature causes water production scores to increase over time and does so without impacting any of the boxes' physical/generational characteristics."

"But it *has* to impact those characteristics," the researchers insist. "A box's physical/generational characteristics embody its water production ability, and therefore embody its usefulness too."

"No, that's just it," the visitor answers. "Those physical/generational characteristics tell only half the story at best. If you want to fully understand the nature of water production ability, as well as fully understand the nature of usefulness, you must also take into account the ambient temperature. And if it's the *increase* in water production ability you're trying to explain, then *all* the focus has to go towards the ambient temperature, because that's the only factor that changes over time."

The researchers are polite but end the discussion by saying they cannot argue established fact—plus they have to get back to combining explanations and attending to impressive mathematical formulas.

The above analogy forms a nearly exact isomorphism to the current situation regarding intelligence and the Flynn effect.

IQ scores are like water production scores, and individual people (or individual brains, if you will) are like boxes. Scientists have built up a large and compelling cache of evidence that variations in IQ scores among individuals are driven by a presumed set of neuronal/genetic characteristics, the idea being that if researchers had good knowledge of an individual's neuronal/genetic background, they would be able to predict within a reasonable degree of accuracy the individual's intelligence score and the corresponding likelihood of success within the community. The correlations are not always exact but they are strong enough to be informative across both individuals and groups.

If that is all there were to it, then intelligence would be essentially explained. However, that is not all there is to it. In addition to the experimental evidence outlined so far, scientists have also discovered that raw intelligence scores keep increasing over time, a phenomenon that has been named the Flynn effect. Intelligence scores keep increasing each year and they keep increasing for essentially every population.

Many explanations for the Flynn effect have been proposed and investigated. Many of these explanations focus on possible improvements to humanity's neuronal/genetic underpinnings—through better nutrition for instance, or assortative mating. Other explanations target specific changes to the human environment, such as increasing amounts of visual stimulation or broader access to advanced education. However all these explanations have only limited scope, and therefore none have been able to account for the ubiquitous and relentless reach of the Flynn effect. Plus the environmental explanations have been perceived as suffering from a still further difficulty, namely that they must be translated into more or less permanent changes in a person's neuronal/genetic characteristics, because everyone agrees that those neuronal/genetic characteristics are what ultimately underlie intelligence. The translation often seems implausible.

Dickens and Flynn (2001) have attempted to solve this dilemma by demonstrating that neuronal/genetic characteristics and environmental factors can resonate off each other with amplifying effect. They have introduced concepts such as social multipliers and feedback loops and have developed complex mathematical formulas to show how their mechanism can be tuned to experimental results. Other researchers, perhaps frustrated over the lack of a definitive answer, have suggested that the Flynn effect cannot be explained by any one factor alone, but that instead a large *combination* of factors must ultimately be brought to bear.

The essay *The Flynn Effect's Unseen Hand* proposes an entirely different approach to the problem, suggesting that the perceived difficulty in solving the Flynn effect is actually being produced by a widespread misunderstanding of the problem's context, in particular by a widespread misunderstanding of what constitutes intelligence. The essay defines the term *environmental intelligence* as the total amount of non-biological pattern, structure and form tangibly contained within the human environment and associates human intelligence to this ambient pattern, structure and form, and repudiates the notion that intelligence must be invariably tied to the workings of the human brain. That there has been a steady increase in *environmental intelligence* can be seen readily enough from a survey of human history: from the beginnings of the human great leap forward, through the transformations of the agricultural revolution, through the development of civilizations such as Mesopotamia, Egypt and Greece, through the fast-paced innovations of the Renaissance, and finally culminating in the explosion of technologies and constructions that humans encounter today. As humans have progressed through their many changing epochs, they have been navigating an increasingly complex framework of pattern, structure and form, and they have been navigating this framework at a faster and faster pace.

This increasing amount of pattern, structure and form makes for an ideal and elegant explanation of the Flynn effect, it has all the essential characteristics. For one, the increase mirrors the increase in raw intelligence scores. Two, the increase in *environmental intelligence* is continuous over time, just as with the rise in test results. Three, the increase in *environmental intelligence* is ubiquitous, people are exposed to it everywhere nearly the same. And finally, in considering the *content* of an intelligence exam—all those questions formed out of pattern, structure and form—one recognizes that navigating an intelligence exam is not unlike navigating the framework of the surrounding world, and thus it cannot be all that surprising that ambient pattern, structure and form must have something to do with human intelligence.

The situation can be described like this: there are three different quantities in play—a person's neuronal/genetic capacity for intelligence, the raw intelligence score, and the total amount of pattern, structure and form contained within the human environment. Letters can be used to stand for these quantities:

C = a person's neuronal/genetic CAPACITY for intelligence,
S = the raw intelligence SCORE, and
T = the TOTAL AMOUNT of pattern, structure and form contained within the human environment.

A person's raw intelligence score (S) is the combination of the two other factors (C and T) working independently. This can be expressed in a simple relationship:

$$S = C \times T.$$

This relationship fits the experimental results perfectly. At any given point in time, the total amount of ambient pattern, structure and form (T) will be constant, so that when experiments are run at that time, all the variation in intelligence scores (S) will be the direct result of the differing neuronal/genetic characteristics of each person, because those neuronal/genetic characteristics are what drive a person's relative capacity (C) to demonstrate intelligence.

But *over* time it is the orthogonal effect that holds sway. Over time, it is C that remains constant; scientists have little in the way of evidence to suggest that profound neuronal/genetic changes occur over time, just as to be expected under the tenets of biology and evolution. But if C remains essentially constant, then all the increase in S over time is explained solely by an increase in T. The increasing amount of pattern, structure and form contained within the human environment causes intelligence scores to go up over time and does so without impacting any person's neuronal/genetic characteristics.

Scientists have a hard time considering, let alone accepting, this new description of intelligence because scientists are working under a mistaken assumption. Their evidence has been so strong and compelling that variations in neuronal/genetic characteristics lead to corresponding differences in intelligence scores that the scientists have somehow become convinced that the inference is valid also in the other direction—that is, that every change in intelligence score is necessarily accompanied by a change in neuronal/genetic characteristics. That unsupported assumption is what leads everyone astray. For instance, all the complexity of the Dickens-Flynn model is being driven by a perceived need to have environmental influences and neuronal/genetic characteristics *interact*. But in reality that interaction is not called for at all, all the evidence clearly indicates that environment influences and neuronal/genetic characteristics are essentially independent.

If there is one disruptive consequence to this new and straightforward accounting of the Flynn effect, it is that it compels a complete reassessment of the word *intelligence*. Because of the perceived (and mistaken) bi-directional linkage of IQ scores and neuronal/genetic characteristics, scientists have been restricting use of the word *intelligence* to the domain of that linkage alone. But neuronal/genetic characteristics tell only half the story at best. If scientists hope to understand fully and accurately the nature of intelligence, then they must also take into account the total amount of non-biological pattern, structure and form tangibly contained within the human environment. And if it is the *increase* in intelligence that scientists are trying to explain, then *all* their focus must go towards the structural human surroundings, because that is the only factor that changes over time.

Animal Intelligence

Chimpanzees communicating with sign language and lexigrams. Rhesus macaques accurately adding Arabic numerals. Dolphins employing sponges as protective gear during foraging. Crows bending wires into food hooks. Octopi transporting and manipulating coconut shells for camouflage and shelter. These and many similar examples are showcased regularly by today's scientists as the evidence that animals—meaning the animal species other than *Homo sapiens*—possess intelligence, intelligence comparable to and in some cases rivaling that of humans.

But when these examples are examined not for what they are *supposed* to demonstrate, but instead for what they *actually* demonstrate, they contradict the scientists' conclusion. What these examples reveal instead is a widespread misunderstanding of what intelligence is. Applied to all but one species on this planet, the phrase *animal intelligence* is essentially meaningless, it forms a null set. And applied to the only exception, applied to the human species, the phrase *animal intelligence* is more akin to a contradiction in terms, a left-to-right juxtaposition of the species' sudden and unprecedented turn from the first word of the phrase to the second.

The many purported examples of animal intelligence fall invariably into one of just two categories.

The first category of animal intelligence consists of those instances typically originated in the laboratory, such as primates displaying language skills and numeracy, birds employing an assortment of knick-knacks as tools, rodents navigating ever-more complex mazes, etc. And more broadly, this first category also encompasses the many domesticated animals, along with their activities that are typically described as intelligent, such as responding to a called name or consistently unlatching the hook from the pen. These types of behavior, when performed by humans, are taken as instances of human intelligence, and so it is an obvious next step to assess similar behaviors, when performed by animals, as instances of animal intelligence. Further boosting this line of reasoning is the widespread assumption that human intelligence is produced via the human brain. Animals clearly have brains too, and so what could be more natural than to characterize an animal's sophisticated laboratory or domestication-based behavior as an expression of an animal intelligence produced via the animal brain. What then arises from all these seemingly straightforward considerations is the widely held belief that not just humans but all the other animals too possess a neural proclivity for intelligence, and although this intelligence might differ in degree from species to species (for presumably evolutionary reasons), it certainly does not differ in kind.

Nonetheless, this line of reasoning masks a crucial omission: it too conveniently forgets the *context* of all these examples. By definition, every instance of a laboratory or domestication-based animal intelligence behavior manifests exclusively within an artificial environment, which is to say that it manifests exclusively under *human*-generated conditions. Chimpanzees do not respond to chimpanzee-invented words and lexigrams, they respond instead to human-invented words and lexigrams. Crows do not manipulate crow-generated artifacts, they manipulate human-generated artifacts. Rats do not navigate rat-engineered mazes, they navigate human-engineered mazes. The inevitable presence and influence of human features within the setting of all these examples calls immediately into question the applicability of the phrase *animal intelligence*, because it remains highly doubtful that *animal* has anything to do with these cases. It might be more legitimate to say that the animals in these examples are displaying not a form of animal intelligence so much as they are simply redisplaying well-known forms of human intelligence, a kind of intelligence irrevocably tied to human-specific circumstances. The distinction is not merely semantic, because in fact its *consequences* are both consistent and real. Without exception, when the human-originated features are removed from the setting of any one of these examples, the corresponding intelligence behaviors disappear right along with them. No primate ever employs an abstract symbol or lexigram in the wild. No cat answers to its given name in the great outdoors.

More tellingly, the presence of human-like animal intelligence behaviors within artificial settings, and the complete absence of such behaviors within natural settings, assails the very notion of an intelligence produced via the brain, be it animal brain or human brain. The fundamental distinction between wild animals and animals brought under human influence is not genetic or neural—the genetic and neural underpinnings remain exactly the same in each case—and so the question needs to be asked, if laboratory and domestication-based animal intelligence behaviors are the evidence of a capacity for intelligence within the animal brain, then why does this capacity not express itself within non-artificial settings? If for instance the primate brain possesses enough intelligence to produce abstract language and arithmetic within the laboratory, then it certainly possesses enough intelligence to produce abstract language and arithmetic within the jungle—and yet it never does so. And thus it would be a logical mistake to attribute animal intelligence behaviors to the animal brain, because in fact the animal brain does not differ from setting to setting, while animal intelligence behaviors can differ *vastly* from setting to setting.

A more logical and more direct explanation for these differing behaviors would be to attribute human-like animal intelligence behaviors to what is actually *distinct* between the circumstances of the laboratory and the circumstances of the wild, namely the presence of human-generated artifacts and influences within the former setting and the complete absence of such artifacts and influences within the latter setting. The human-originated environment—mostly non-biological, highly constructed, and abundantly suffused with underlying elements of pattern, symmetry, repetition, structure and form—this is the only distinguishing feature to which to attribute human-like animal intelligence behaviors, behaviors that manifest within its presence but disappear upon its absence. The human context, the human *intelligence* context, cannot be overlooked in the description of laboratory and domestication-based animal intelligence behaviors, because it is this context alone that emerges as the precipitating factor for the induction of such behaviors.

Furthermore, since human-like animal intelligence behaviors can be attributed solely to the presence of artificial and structural features within the surrounding environment of such behaviors—and cannot be attributed to the animal brain—there is little reason to expect the situation is any different for humans themselves. It is of course not possible to observe directly the comparable behaviors of modern humans versus wild humans (even the few remaining humans yet living under primitive conditions are still thoroughly surrounded from birth in artificial features and circumstances—abstract language, weapons, constructed shelters, etc.). Nonetheless, the evidence from anthropological history reveals that for a very long period of time *Homo sapiens* individuals lived as little more than animals themselves, engaged almost entirely in a struggle for survival and procreation. And if one were to compare the language, arithmetic, tool usage, shelter creation and other intelligence behaviors between those ancient humans and modern humans, one would recognize that here too, just as was the case in the comparison of wild animals versus laboratory and domestication-based animals, the gulf in intelligence behaviors is vast—a nearly complete *absence* in the former case and an overwhelming *presence* in the latter. But unless one is prone to believe in biological or evolutionary magic, one cannot attribute this vast gulf in intelligence behaviors to genetic or neural causes, because in fact the genetic and neural distinction between those ancient humans and modern humans is minuscule, negligible, essentially a comparison of a species against itself. Instead, the only differentiating influence to which to attribute the vast gulf in intelligence behaviors between ancient humans and modern humans is the large and obvious distinction in their environmental circumstances. For ancient humans, their immediate surroundings were as natural as natural can be, void of all artificial constructs and features, the equivalent of a wild animal's domain; while for modern humans the natural world has been practically eclipsed from view, crowded out by surroundings that are mostly non-biological, highly constructed, and abundantly suffused with underlying characteristics of pattern, symmetry, repetition, structure and form. For modern humans, the source and inspiration of their many and varied intelligence behaviors can be found literally everywhere close at hand, while for ancient humans such sources and inspirations were literally nowhere to be seen, and this vast difference in setting, coupled with a near equivalence in biological underpinning, strongly challenges the notion of a human intelligence produced via the human brain.

Thus for this first category of examples offered in support of the existence of an animal intelligence—examples originated in the laboratory, the barnyard and the home—it can be seen that the widespread and unquestioned assumption that such behaviors are the evidence of an animal intelligence produced via the animal brain overlooks what these examples actually convey. The presence of such behaviors exclusively in human-originated circumstances means that this form of intelligence is more *human* inspired than it is *animal* inspired, and means that far from being produced via the animal brain—a brain that is just as functional and just as present in the wild—these intelligence behaviors are more directly attributable to the human-centric features and influences that constitute the behaviors' surrounding environment, the only type of environment in which these behaviors manifest.

The second category of examples offered as evidence for animal intelligence reverses the circumstances of the first. The second category of animal intelligence consists solely of those cases that occur entirely within natural surroundings, completely removed from any artificial (that is to say, human) influence. This includes instances such as dolphins and mollusks employing found objects for shelter and tool, migratory birds navigating by landmarks and stars, squirrels employing deception to safeguard their cache of food, etc. Indeed the enumeration of examples from this second category of animal intelligence would appear to be potentially without end, because it could reasonably be argued that *any* behavior successfully advancing an animal's quest for survival and procreation could be a candidate for inclusion in this category. Scientists are apt to concentrate only on those behaviors that have a similarity to well-known human behaviors—behaviors that are considered by the scientists to be humanly intelligent—but this clearly reflects some anthropocentric bias and effectively reduces the phrase *animal intelligence* as applied to this second category to be little more than a synonym for *animal similarity to modern humanness*. Yet even under the influence of this anthropocentric bias, much of the ambiguity would still remain. For although a human might cleverly apply deception to safeguard his valuables in certain circumstances, he might also smartly employ brute force when different circumstances arise; and so when the squirrel protects its stash of acorns via deception within the tree and the lion preserves its kill via brute force upon the savanna, are both behaviors to be described as intelligent?

In this second category of animal intelligence, quite in contrast to the first, the phrase *animal intelligence* is no longer controversial with regard to its first word, but the controversy now rages full tilt around the suitability of the second word. Since all the examples within this category reflect natural behaviors, behaviors that have been forged through evolution and that have become well ingrained into the species, what justifies the application of the word *intelligence* to particular instances of these behaviors, and how would these particular instances be distinguished (could they be distinguished) from all the other natural behaviors that effectively serve the purpose of advancing an animal's quest for survival and procreation?

This much should be for certain: if the standard use of the word *intelligence* within scientific discourse is to be given any weight at all, then there is no question it is a *definitional mistake* to apply the word *intelligence* to any biologically natural behavior, be it successful or otherwise, and be it similar to human behavior or not. This is seen most clearly and most directly by inspecting the *contents* of that preeminent tool for measuring intelligence, the IQ exam. Although this feature is often overlooked, an IQ exam deliberately and categorically excludes many types of behavior from its jurisdiction. For instance, a test-taker's athletic ability never comes into play—one's ability to run, leap or throw neither helps nor hinders one's performance on an IQ exam. And more germane to the discussion at hand, an IQ exam never assesses a test-taker's ability to survive or procreate under primitive conditions—one's ability to vanquish predator or prey and one's likelihood to foster a prodigious lineage neither helps nor hinders one's performance on an IQ exam. What an IQ exam does measure is a circumscribed and biologically foreign set of capabilities and behaviors, targeting a test-taker's capacity to respond productively to a series of challenges constructed almost entirely out of artificial components, components carrying the underlying characteristics of pattern, symmetry, repetition, structure and form. It is by these circumscribed and biologically foreign means that an IQ exam can capture the type of human-like intelligence behavior that was the focus of attention under the first category of examples offered in support of animal intelligence, but it is also by these same means that an IQ exam *excludes* the type of biologically natural behavior that is the focus of attention under this second category of animal intelligence. By design and by intent, biologically natural behaviors are to have no influence on intelligence as measured by an IQ exam, and thus any resemblance of natural behaviors to behaviors that *are* measurable by an IQ exam must be taken as little more than accidental coincidence.

In addition, the *fluidity* of an IQ exam's contents, along with the corresponding fluidity of what those contents measure, provides still more justification for uncoupling intelligence behaviors, which are quite malleable, from biologically natural behaviors, which are not malleable at all. For instance, it has been well documented that due to the Flynn effect intelligence exams must be re-engineered on a regular basis, recasting questions to be more sophisticated and more challenging as time goes on.

Questions assessing a test-taker's general knowledge, which would have been quite localized in the past, today must encompass a global, indeed a universal, scale; and questions covering topics such as mathematics, logic, vocabulary and grammar would have looked quite different if set hundreds of years ago versus how they are set today, and will morph still further when presented in the future (think for instance of the manner in which electronic communication is altering the rules of vocabulary and grammar even today). Plus it is not just the shifting nature of the IQ exam that attests to this fluidity of intelligence; in everyday usage and in general application it can be seen that intelligence behaviors have an inherent tendency to transition over time. A human of the past who could use his scythe to harvest grain would have been described as reasonably intelligent, but today's farmer who cannot advance beyond the scythe to the mechanisms of the combine will be assessed as far less so, and the engineer of the future who cannot transcend both the scythe and the combine to master the intricacies of the automated process will be seen as intellectually left behind. In short, intelligence behaviors do not stand still, they do not solidify into long-term habit or an enduring nature. Intelligence behaviors are generalizable, they can be quickly advanced. Intelligence behaviors are promulgated rapidly and then widely transformed.

By contrast, biologically natural behaviors are characterized precisely by the fact they have become so deeply ingrained, the predictable and enduring aspects of the species in particular and of the animal kingdom in general. Forged through evolution and constrained by biological pressures, natural behaviors transform on only the rarest of occasions and under the most extreme of circumstances. Almost every offered example of animal intelligence that falls within the domain of this second category—dolphins employing sponges as tools, birds navigating by landmarks, intricate nest building, insect communication dances, coordinated pack hunting, etc.— every one of these behaviors would have been observable exactly as it is today a hundred thousand years ago, and will be observable exactly as it is today a hundred thousand years into the future, with no generalization, no advancement, no promulgation, no transformation. If there were exams for measuring the capacity for any of these natural behaviors, the exams would never need to be revised but could serve their purpose faithfully millennium after millennium after millennium.

One of the more prominent examples of this tendency to mistake an ingrained natural behavior for an intelligence behavior comes from the history of humans themselves, in their use of stone tools. Although widely accepted as at least a precursor to intelligence, the ancient employment of edged choppers went nonetheless ungeneralized and unchanged for hundreds of thousands of years and thus was more akin to something like nest building in the birds than to anything artificial or modern. It was not until the human tool set suddenly transformed, transformed in material and categorization (and quite recently in human history and accompanied by dozens of other behavioral changes) that the species found itself rapidly rearranging its environmental circumstances and marching hurriedly towards an intelligence age. If there were a man today who could master no more than the flaking of some flint while at the same time being utterly dumbfounded by hammers, pliers and awls, he would not be regarded as intelligent, and neither would his long line of descendants if they were to somehow become stuck on these same stone choppers generation after generation after generation.

In comparison to biologically natural behaviors, intelligence behaviors are strange, fleeting and foreign, traveling almost exclusively in the company of artificial constructs. Intelligence behaviors share essentially none of the enduring evolutionary characteristics that define biologically natural behaviors. Intelligence behaviors are not driven solely by a need for survival and procreation, intelligence behaviors do not become deeply entrenched, and intelligence behaviors were nowhere to be seen on this planet until humans quite recently and quite suddenly and quite prodigiously took them on. The many purported examples of animal intelligence that fall within this second category are in fact *contradictions* to the word *intelligence*, their biological and evolutionary underpinning meaning *ipso facto* they are to be excluded. That these instances are so frequently cited as examples of animal intelligence can be attributed primarily to a cause that is both obvious and quite benign, namely that these examples bear an accidental resemblance to modern human behaviors, and scientists are unable to suppress their anthropocentric bias.

Thus for the animal species other than *Homo sapiens*, the phrase *animal intelligence* finds no meaningful application, its legitimate instances forming a null set. All the examples that would fall under the first category of animal intelligence, examples originated in artificial settings, fail on the word *animal*. And all the examples that would fall under the second category of animal intelligence, examples originated in natural settings, fail on the word *intelligence*. On Earth, the phrase *animal intelligence* currently attaches to humans and to humans alone.

Nonetheless, even with humans the phrase *animal intelligence* has the most uneasy and paradoxical application, its two words representing two fundamental and opposing aspects of human nature. Indeed modern humans might be more articulately described by the phrase *animal versus intelligence*. This conflict arose of course historically, for man was once nothing more than animal himself and like the other species was a complete stranger to intelligence, a complete stranger to any artificial construct composed out of pattern, symmetry, repetition, structure or form. In those ancient yet not-so-long-ago days (not so long ago, that is, on any biological or geographical timescale), evolution was still the primary master, and the quest for survival and procreation was still the sole motivator. But today, for modern humans, the tables have been nearly turned: nature has been practically eclipsed from view, survival and procreation have been mostly tamed by artificial means, and the evolutionary process has been turned completely on its head. The great unanswered scientific question of the present day (a question only humans are capable of asking) is how to describe and explain this sudden and prodigious transformation—what are its characteristics, what brought it about, and what are its ultimate consequences?

The popular and conventional explanation for modern humans and their burgeoning intelligence is to claim everything must have arisen as an evolutionary event. Some would describe this event as gradual, to meet the requirements of biological and evolutionary principles, and others— Richard Klein, for instance—would describe this event as sudden, to meet the requirements of mankind's surprisingly rapid turn. But in any case the necessary requirement would seem to be that human intelligence be depicted primarily as a product of biological evolution, something akin to a genetic mutation producing a cascading neurological effect, because of course *all* animal transformations are products of evolution, are they not, can there really be such a thing as an exception?

But in fact intelligence *is* the exception. Not *an* exception, but the *essential* exception. Intelligence contravenes evolution, intelligence is thoroughly anti-evolutionary in its process, cause and effect. On Earth, man with his newfound intelligence has become an anti-evolutionary creature, an anti-evolutionary force, producing astounding environmental impact, observable literally everywhere close at hand.

Most of the grounds for this determination have already been stated. When describing the circumstances in which intelligence behaviors, be they human or animal, exclusively manifest, it was noted that intelligence behaviors always appear within *artificial* settings and are always attached to *constructed* circumstances. Intelligence performance is measured primarily by an *artificial* instrument, its content composed entirely out of *forged* components, its domain enjoined from measuring any athletic or primeval ability. When comparing intelligence behaviors to biologically natural behaviors, it was noted that intelligence behaviors are fluid and accumulative, not conservative and ingrained, and that intelligence changes are predictable via generalization and rapid promulgation, not random, as is the case with geological and gene mutative events. These already stated observations can be summarized into one readily apparent fact: the characteristics of intelligence are *incompatible* with the characteristics of biology and nature, the characteristics of intelligence are diametrically *opposed* to the characteristics of evolution.

This fact becomes even more apparent when comparing the dynamics that underlie intelligence and evolution. Evolutionary dynamics are well known and straightforward to describe. Given a stable environment, organisms, as the genetic representatives of their species, undergo selection for that environment through a striving for survival and procreation. The organisms which are best suited to the environment will more likely emerge as dominant and established, and the organisms which are less suited to the environment will more likely diminish by being dominated and crowded out. Environmental change will foster some transition and churn, as will random genetic mutation, but since significant environmental change tends to be rare in typical circumstances and since random genetic mutation tends to face long odds for increasing environmental fit, evolution is usually a conservative and slow-moving process, with significant alteration often taking place on the scale of hundreds of thousands or even millions of years.

The dynamics underlying intelligence are composed of these exact same components—environment, selection, mutation, survival and procreation—but these components are rearranged into a contrasting pattern, producing a fast-moving process that runs in evolution's counter-direction. Intelligence begins with just one species, a species that will not undergo any significant genetic mutation. The organisms of this species, once subject to natural selection like all the other species, begin to *circumvent* selection by substituting instead its artificial counterpart, selectively mutating the organisms' environment, mutating it in such a way as to make the surrounding conditions more supportive of the organisms' survival and procreation (and generally less supportive of neighboring species' survival and procreation). The key to this deliberate, non-natural environmental mutation is an awareness of the environment's underlying characteristics, characteristics that are mostly non-biological and that are abundantly suffused with elements of pattern, symmetry, repetition, structure and form. The organisms of this species make use of these characteristics to mutate their environment in a self-preserving manner—think clothing, shelter, weapons, abstract words—and these tangible mutations serve also as the prominent, long-lasting embodiment of the underlying characteristics themselves, helping spread their influence to the other members of the species. And since these non-biological environmental mutations are not subject to any genetic or geological constraint, they can be implemented with accumulating impact and increasing speed, a feature currently being demonstrated by humankind on a nearly daily basis.

Thus to make use of intelligence is to *defy* evolution; a species acquiring intelligence is turning evolution on its head. Or to make the comparison more direct: with evolution, the environment selects among mutating organisms for the best environmental fit, while with intelligence (anti-evolution), the organism selects among mutable environments for the best organism fit. Evolution and intelligence are *opposing* forces, they run in *counter* directions.

The recent history of *Homo sapiens* might tempt one to think that in the conflict between evolutionary animal and anti-evolutionary intelligence, intelligence must be emerging as the victor. Humans have been moving further and further away from their former animal circumstances and now live in settings where the artificial features outnumber the natural features on a scale of perhaps a hundred to one, or maybe even a thousand to one. Intelligence has been measurably increasing population wide year after year (the Flynn effect), and intelligence has grown so copious that a good portion of its augmentation is no longer directed to survival and procreation (understanding of the Big Bang for instance, intriguing as it might be, is not likely to impact human continuance anytime soon). The human transformation has been charting what seems to be a direct and inevitable course, straight from all animal and no intelligence to all intelligence and no animal.

But such a conclusion would be illusory. The abundant increase in human intelligence, admittedly quite real, masks a reality that is just as important and just as essential, namely that the animal in man has gone nowhere at all, man's animal nature has diminished not one bit. The primary justification for this verdict is of course the fact that the requirements of survival and procreation still remain in full effect. Although intelligence and its many constructions have certainly eased the immediate challenges of survival and procreation for most people, and have sheltered the human species from a broad array of biological contingencies, these protections are nonetheless fragile and increasingly complex, and therefore not guaranteed to last. Nuclear arsenals, the profligate destruction of climate, eradication of supporting species, plus hundreds of other unseen vicissitudes—ruinous catastrophe seems to lurk around nearly every bend and along with it a return, at best, to an ancient and bestial existence. But even discounting this potential for civilization collapse, even assuming circumstances will continue as is, man's animal heritage must still insist on having its say. Greed, lust, rivalries, nepotism, revenge—these easily traceable holdovers from man's primate beginnings serve not only as the most captivating plot devices in popular forms of modern entertainment, they serve also as the most compelling motivators of day-to-day action in a modern human society. So resilient has been the primitive impulse within human temperament that the efforts of intelligence have often been the most successful not when *confronting* the lingering animal within man but instead when assimilating it, even sublimating it, and thereby channeling much of its pent-up energy. Anyone who has ever witnessed up close the inner workings of a modern corporation, and has experienced first-hand the often devious and sometimes brutal scramble towards executive office and boardroom key, will have a perfect acquaintance with the vestigial characteristics of a hierarchical clan. Anyone who has ever attended the clamorous and furious taking up of sides in the giant arenas of battle—the home warriors clashing against the invading marauders—will have an intimate familiarity with the fears accompanying territorial battle and will have rediscovered a hunger for the spoils of conquest. Even when intelligence has been at its most powerful and progressive, even when building sophisticated constructions capable of advancing the entirety of the human species, intelligence has been nonetheless helpless against the species' more visceral traits permeating the final results. Witness one of the more recent triumphs of intelligence, witness the development of widespread electronic communication, capable of spreading advancement to literally the entire human population, and then witness the most popular and frequent use of that instrument, as the preferred and efficient conduit of gossip, fraud and pornography.

Some humans will no doubt feel an urge to pull back towards humanity's more familiar animal past, not comprehending that such a retreat would mean a return to the exigencies and stasis of a primordial existence. Other humans will desire that the forces of intelligence ultimately conquer the animal within man, not recognizing that such an outcome would threaten an end to all vitality. What remains elusive is the *purpose* behind the introduction of intelligence into an animal species, what could be its *telos*, but whatever that purpose or *telos* might be, the fundamental conflict so engendered appears to be at its most productive only while it is being waged and not when it is being won. The fate of modern humans is irrevocably tied to this ongoing struggle between animal and intelligence—between evolution and anti-evolution—and it is in this context, and in this context only, that the phrase *animal intelligence* acquires legitimate and substantive meaning.

Conspecifics

What makes a biological species such an intriguing concept is its stasis. From out of a near maelstrom of biological and evolutionary dynamics—selection, genetics, generation—a species emerges as something obstinately distinct, stable and enduring. Darwin himself was puzzled that nature does not formulate instead into a mishmash of morphologies and traits, with a more gradual and more frequent variation across space and across time. This puzzlement, an aspect of what is often referred to as *Darwin's dilemma,* has never been completely resolved. The modern explanations for nature's tendency to coalesce into well-delineated and persistent species usually center around such notions as reproductive isolation and costs of rarity, but in many respects these accounts miss a good deal of the point, because a species is not only static and conservative in its morphology and reproductive viability, a species is also static and conservative in its overall behavior, to the point of being almost perfectly predictable across the entirety of its existence. If for instance one were to film a documentary about almost any plant or animal species, place the film inside a vault for a hundred thousand years, one could then retrieve the documentary and present it as still accurate and up to date, with scarcely the need for a single edit. This dogged constancy across the entire reach of the phylogenetic network appears to be the evidence of an underlying biological invariance, a law if you will, a law that has not been adequately determined.

And to make the matter still more puzzling, there is the one notable exception to the law—the one case of the law having encountered a blatant violator. That is to say, the human species.

Humanity certainly did not *begin* as the most obvious counterexample to the law of species stasis. The genus *Homo* and its predecessors had for millions of years been unfolding into an entirely standard set of stable and generally durable groupings: *afarensis, africanus, habilis, ergaster, erectus, heidelbergensis, neanderthalensis*. And for quite some time *Homo sapiens* too appeared to be slated for the same usual course, its members passing through typical and mostly unvarying animal lives within the more hospitable corners of the African continent. But it was around fifty thousand years ago that an unprecedented behavioral transformation began to take shape within the species, a transformation that has only accelerated throughout the intervening years and today shows no signs of abatement. In the early twenty-first century almost no characteristic of human behavior would be recognizable to anyone who could have observed or recorded man's earlier days on the savanna. And although it is indeed behavior that constitutes the most clear-cut difference between the humans of today and the humans of the past, with the advent of everything from dental implants to artificial knees, from Viagra to augmented bosoms, from in vitro fertilization to stem cell technologies, it is evident that much of the morphological and reproductive intransigence still lingering within the human species is now on the verge of disappearing as well.

And thus there are two fundamental questions to be investigated regarding the concept of a biological species. One, what compels a species, across all its generations, to maintain such consistent and stable behavior? And two, how is it that the human species has managed to escape this compulsion?

To better understand the reasons for the widespread stability underlying species behavior, perhaps the best place to begin is with a depiction that might not seem at first to be all that related—namely the philosophy of Immanuel Kant. But Kant was the first to fully confront the challenge of describing how a persistent biological consciousness can arise from the continuous multitude of sensory impressions that each organism receives, impressions that in their rawest form would be little more than chaotic and overwhelming, would be little more than useless noise. One of the goals of the *Critique of Pure Reason* was to outline the process whereby sensory impressions can transcend their inherent chaos and become the basis for effective and consistent behavior. And although Kant's approach, including his heavy reliance upon syllogistic logic, was perhaps not entirely adequate to the task, Kant's groundbreaking effort still managed to capture the essence of what would have to be incorporated into *any* proposed solution to the problem of biological consciousness, namely a recognition that in order for consciousness to arise at all, an organism's multitude of sensory impressions would have to be *unified* under some kind of structure or rule. Or to put it in the parlance of modern data science, each organism's raw sensory input would have to be sorted, filtered, mapped and reduced, resulting finally in the kind of perceptual foregrounding and targeted awareness that could serve as the basis for productive action. Kant's depiction is too often taken to be merely philosophical or as applicable to human reasoning alone, but in fact it is the most informative when applied biologically: the early pages of the *Critique of Pure Reason* outline a general framework whereby a manifold of biological *stimulus* can be transformed into precise and targeted *response*—something no lion on the prowl could ever do without.

Kant was also the first to recognize that the *means* of any sorting, filtering, mapping and reducing would have to be provided by the organism itself, and that the general *form* of these means would be the primary determinant of the organism's perceptual content, and therefore the primary determinant of the organism's resulting behavior. Kant often used the somewhat vague and magical-sounding term *faculty* to highlight these organism-provided means, but of course it has to be remembered that Kant was writing well before the advent of Darwin, Mendel and an accurate rendition of Earth's biological timeline—so some vagueness and magic are to be excused. Today, post the advent of Darwin, Mendel and an accurate rendition of Earth's biological timeline, the *a priori* means that underlie sensory unification and perceptual foregrounding are now more richly detailed and more deeply understood, having shed their vagueness upon a wealth of observable information regarding biochemistry and genetics, and having cast off their magical aura behind a well-described evolutionary process that spans hundreds of millions of years. In the biological kingdom, what drives the means for sorting, filtering, mapping and reducing, what shapes the structure and rule behind stimulus unification and targeted response, are the ongoing requirements of survival and procreation—physically manifested within each organism's biochemical structure and honed into effectiveness through enormously long stretches of selection and generation.

The capstone of Kant's description, his list of conceptual categories—organized under such headings as quality, quantity, modality, plurality and negation—was arrived at in an attempt to achieve maximum generality.

But in a certain sense, all this ardent abstraction vastly overshoots the mark when applied to a biological context, where really only concreteness will do. Because if one were to search from the treetops of the Amazonian rain forests all the way to the depths of the ocean floor, it would be a frustrating endeavor to find anywhere a biological consciousness unified around such notions as quality, quantity, modality, plurality or negation. And yet by contrast, it would be little more than child's play to find a biological consciousness unified around such categories as food, water, danger, shelter, family, sex, predators, prey, conspecifics. In the *experienced* world, it is concrete biological need that determines the primary structure of biological perception, and it is the pervasive and unyielding impetus behind these biologically determined categories that provides the primary reason for why biological behavior remains so consistent and stable. In the *experienced* world, survival ceaselessly asserts its decrees, procreation fervently presses its demands, evolution ruthlessly carries out its mandate. Each organism, both outwardly and inwardly, must adhere to these strict regulations or else disappear. And so in a broad and inexorable lockstep, the members of the biological community must aim their rapt and conscious attention towards food, water, danger, shelter, family, sex, predators, prey, conspecifics—and then each must respond accordingly, and thus each responds mostly the same.

Of the biologically determined categories, conspecific awareness and recognition holds special significance. It is the primary catalyst, at least within the animal kingdom, behind each species developing a strong tendency to coalesce—both territorially and behaviorally. Each organism possesses a predisposition to foreground first and foremost those sensory impressions that are directly associated with the other members of its own species; lions perceive and attend primarily to other lions, geese perceive and attend predominantly to other geese, ants perceive and attend chiefly to other ants (and of course humans perceive and attend first and foremost to other humans). The principal inducement towards this nearly universal characteristic of an intra-species awareness is that it is the most direct solution to what would otherwise be a haphazard reproductive challenge. Successful mating requires that the male and female conjoin at the same time and same location, a rendezvous that would be made problematic, if not downright impossible, should each member of the species be unable to distinguish and foreground its own kind from all the remainder. Even in those rare instances where organisms live solitary lives, and egg-laying and fertilization are separated significantly in time, the species is still bound together by the perceptual foregrounding of the expected *location* of egg-laying and fertilization, an effective proxy for conspecific prominence.

And beyond the logistical requirements of procreation, many species make extensive use of conspecific foregrounding to advance a broad range of beneficial behaviors. Nurturing of the young for instance necessitates that adults carry a perceptual preference for the offspring of their own kind—lest lions find themselves randomly rearing goslings, geese find themselves indiscriminately raising ants, and so on. Successful foraging, pack hunting and herd defense all require a keen perceptual attention to the other members of the population, even when those members occupy no more than a minuscule portion of the entire sensory field. But perhaps most importantly of all, conspecific awareness and recognition allows tried-and-tested species behaviors to be passed along from generation to generation, without the inefficient obligation that each and every behavior be imprinted genetically or be made completely instinctual. The maturing members of many species go through a period of time in which their main occupation is to scrutinize parents, siblings, extended family and other models within the population, imitating observed activities and eventually taking on those activities with an increasing faithfulness (and thereby becoming models for the next generation). This recurrent cycle of learned and transmitted behavior is always confined to the species itself—lions do not learn from leopards, geese do not model sparrows, no organism imitates non-biological objects. Each organism is a fully engaged student of its own kind—and is nearly oblivious to everything else.

Thus the trait of conspecific awareness and recognition has both the powerful and restrictive impact of making a species insular. Conspecific foregrounding encourages a species to cluster, it turns the species' members inwards for mutual protection and predatory assistance, and it promotes generational continuance of the species' more successful behaviors. But the unrelenting narrowness of this characteristic also has the consequence of effectively *blinding* the species to any alternative information that the sensory field might have to offer—whether that information would come from other species or from the non-biological world. Nearly all sensory impressions not directly connected to the species itself, or to the immediate requirements of survival and procreation, are relegated to the sensory background and never gain perceptual prominence, and thus never influence biological attention or behavior. As a result, the species is provided little opportunity or incitement to change, since perceptually speaking, nothing ever differs from generation to generation. So powerful and so confining is the impact of conspecific awareness and recognition that it needs to be considered a fundamental and essential component of the *definition* of a species, because a species is determined not only by its morphological similarities and its reproductive sufficiency, it is also determined by the mutual awareness and recognition among all its members, the glue that holds the species together and assures its unvarying continuance.

Each organism's inherent perceptual inclination towards its conspecific neighbors, along with each organism's corresponding disinclination towards the members of other species, suggests there must be a boundary somewhere between these two extremes. On the near side of the boundary, conspecific awareness and recognition functions within a certain degree of tolerance, for despite there being varying levels of genetic and morphological difference among species members, with no two members forming a perfect genetic or morphological match, conspecific foregrounding still manages to remain effective and active throughout the population, with every member gaining targeted attention and every member receiving prominent recognition. But this tolerance clearly must have its limits. It does not extend so far as to encompass the members of other species, and thus it can be assumed that as the conspecific distance increases between organisms—a function of increased morphological and/or genetic difference—a boundary will eventually be reached where the tolerance becomes fully extended and then finally exceeded, with a corresponding attenuation and loss of any conspecific awareness and recognition.

These concepts of conspecific distance, conspecific tolerance and conspecific boundary play an important role in assessing the expected outcome for any organism introducing genetic alteration into a species. A unique genetic signature carries capacity for a transformed species dynamic, with the degree of uniqueness determining the potential for change. But the mechanisms of conspecific awareness serve to work *against* these species alterations, promoting instead an ongoing conservatism, a conservatism that remains well inside any extant conspecific boundary. It is those species members that carry genetic differences that are insignificant in effect and/or infrequent in number that will be the species members that remain well *inside* the conspecific tolerance range, and it is these same species members that will experience and share typical conspecific foregrounding, along with all the resulting conspecific perceptions and behaviors. And thus it is these same species members that will become the fully participating members of the species community, markedly improving their chances and opportunities for procreation and continuation, preserving nothing more subversive than a few non-transformative mutations. To some extent this scenario plays out with nearly every offspring, because although each organism does possess a genetic signature that is distinct in some degree, in the large majority of instances this distinction will be too insignificant to interfere with conspecific awareness, and will be too insignificant to alter the species dynamic.

In comparison, those species members that carry genetic differences that are potent in effect and/or frequent in number will be the same species members that experience an increased conspecific distance from the remainder of the population, a distance that should it become great enough will strain and surpass the conspecific tolerance range. Such organisms would then be perceptually set adrift, less able to recognize and foreground their population partners, while they in turn would be less able to recognize and foreground it. These circumstances would markedly reduce the chances and opportunities for procreation and continuance, meaning that those genetic alterations that are more likely to transform a species are the same genetic alterations that are more likely to be thwarted. To take an extreme example, one could imagine a lion being born with such an exaggerated level of genetic mutation that it might effectively be deemed a leopard, meaning that this newborn and its "conspecific" lion neighbors would be destined to become perceptual strangers, with the newborn's chances for survival and procreation almost guaranteed to turn nil. But even at a much lesser extreme of conspecific distance, challenging biological consequences can still be anticipated, and thus conspecific distancing almost certainly plays a role in the warding off of significant genetic change, a primary mechanism whereby conspecific recognition contributes to the ongoing stasis of a species.

Although the odds of continuation are indeed negligible for an organism outside the conspecific tolerance range, the prognosis is more ambiguous, and in some ways more intriguing, for an organism *nearing* the conspecific boundary—near enough that conspecific awareness and recognition is weakened to some extent but not so near as to make survival and procreation essentially impossible. There are several distinguishing characteristics that can be predicted for such an organism. Mating for instance, although not precluded, will certainly be more problematic, since the organism's inherent perception for its potential mates, as well as their perception in turn for it, will be more nebulous than is the case for the remainder of the population, leading to courtship behaviors that might seem awkward or strange. In species that make heavy use of conspecific foregrounding for mutual defense and combined attack, any member stretching the conspecific limit will of necessity be a weaker participant in these population activities and might come to be regarded as an encumbrance by way of result. And perhaps most importantly of all, the maturation process for a more conspecifically distanced organism will almost certainly be more difficult and more delayed than for the majority of its peers, the relative inability and disinclination to scrutinize others in the population and to imitate their behaviors hampering the typical transmission of species behaviors. Such an organism would not only genetically become an outlier to the population, it would also perceptually and behaviorally become an outlier as well.

For such an organism, however, there is a potential compensation. Recalling the lessons from Kant, it needs to be noted again that the primary purpose behind any form of perception is to unify sensory impressions—impressions that would otherwise remain chaotic, overwhelming and useless. To the extent that an organism's perceptual mechanisms are diminished by its biological circumstances, as would be the case for an organism experiencing an increased conspecific distance, the corresponding unification of sensory experience will be diminished as well. This weakening of sensory unification will give rise to an assortment of sensory difficulties—hypersensitivity, hyposensitivity, synaesthesia. The affected organism, less able to organize its sensory experience around the foregrounded features associated with conspecific awareness and recognition, will find itself struggling with almost every aspect of sensory input. Thus in order to ameliorate these sensory difficulties, a conspecifically distanced organism will be driven towards *alternative* means of sensory unification—which is to say, it will be driven towards alternative means of perception. And it is these alternative means of perception that provide the potential for compensation, because they effectively open the door to a much wider awareness of the entire sensory field, including those features associated with other species, and more significantly, including those features associated with the non-biological world. As it happens, the non-biological world provides a prodigiously rich framework of organizing principles that can serve as the basis for unification of sensory experience—principles that go under such headings as symmetry, repetition, pattern, structure and form. The irony is that these alternative organizing principals are in theory available to *every* organism, but the restrictive impact of biological perception in general, and of conspecific awareness and recognition in particular, pushes awareness of these non-biological features well into the sensory background, and thus it is only those organisms that somehow get *loosened* from the strictures of conspecific awareness and recognition that can thereby gain the opportunity to foreground these alternative features from the surrounding environment, and can thereby gain the potential to achieve a much broader and deeper awareness of the entire sensory field.

If a population were to contain only one such conspecifically distanced organism, or perhaps just a few, then there would likely be little impact on the species as a whole. But if the population were to somehow incorporate a significant number of such organisms, and if that number were to remain stable over a reasonable period of time, then the species dynamic could begin to change. All the necessary conditions for a change would be in place: the broader population would have a conspecific relationship to the population's more distant members (albeit a looser relationship than normal), and the more distant members would have access to a wider array of perceptual experience. The natural workings of conspecific awareness and recognition would prompt the broader population to begin to notice the new behaviors and new perceptions being originated by the more distant members, an awareness that might eventually encourage imitation. In this manner the enhanced perceptual experience of the population's more distant members would begin to infiltrate the perceptual experience of the species as a whole, and with this change in overall species perception would come a corresponding change in overall species behavior. In defiance of the universal expectation of a continual species stasis, this species would be on the verge of a behavioral revolution.

Of course considering the biological fragility that haunts the conspecific boundary, and observing the non-changing behavior of every species currently to be found in the natural world, it would seem that any talk of a behavioral revolution being driven by conspecific distancing would have to be characterized as little more than an academic exercise, as little more than some hypothetical musing. And indeed that would be the end of the discussion if it were not for the one piece of unfinished biological business—namely how to account for that one species that has emerged suddenly and prominently as a blatant violator of the tenets of species stasis, how to account for that one species that has broadly expanded its perceptual experience of the sensory world, how to account for that one species of which it can no longer be said that it can be found in the natural world. How to account for the human species.

The behavioral revolution of the human species has been nothing short of stunning in both its scope and its speed. There is little in the way of evidence to suggest that prior to around fifty thousand years ago *Homo sapiens* individuals lived much differently than all the other animals— riding the ebbs and flows of survival and procreation, gazing out upon an entirely natural landscape, confined to the African continent alone. And then suddenly everything began to change. Art, symbolism, categorized tools, sophisticated weaponry—all began appearing in ever-increasing numbers and with ever-accelerating technique. Humans began to spread geographically and did not stop until the entire planet had been covered. They extincted many other species along the way and bred a chosen few into domesticated abundance. Today, very few humans gaze out upon an entirely natural landscape—artificial environments have become vastly the human norm.

One notable aspect of this human revolution is that it has been accompanied by—indeed it has been *driven* by—a broadened perceptual awareness of the sensory world, and in particular a broadened perceptual awareness of the non-biological world. Nearly all the changes that have become the hallmark features of modern human existence have been built upon a backbone of non-biological constructs, everything from the grammatical patterns of language all the way to the structured symmetries of towering skyscrapers. Literally everywhere one looks, one finds profuse application of the organizing principles of pattern, symmetry, repetition, structure and form—principles that would have never reached the surface of human ken not that long ago, but that today constitute the proliferating and artificial embodiment of man's ever-burgeoning intelligence.

Thus it is that the characteristics of the human behavioral revolution can be seen as matching almost word for word the description given above for a species change brought about by the influence of conspecific distancing. The enormous human *behavioral* change has been accompanied by an equally enormous human *perceptual* change, by an expanded perceptual awareness, one that goes far beyond the restrictions of biological perception alone and one that captures instead an entire panoply of artificial domains. And although humans still retain their conspecific awareness and recognition for one another, and although they still possess sensory instincts for survival and procreation, humans are no longer *constricted* by these biological demands—the human species has been freed almost entirely from its former perceptual prison.

The predictions of conspecific distancing would suggest that this liberation must have been catalyzed through the influence of a significant and stable subpopulation of conspecifically distanced members, human outliers who driven by biological and sensory necessity would have been the first to explore an alternative means of perceiving their sensory world—the species' pathfinders to an expanded form of perception. And thus the question can be asked: within the human population, is there a recognizable subgroup of members who can be seen as possessing the distinguishing behavioral characteristics, including all the inherent challenges, of a conspecifically distanced organism? Are there discernible individuals who evince the telltale weakness in conspecific foregrounding and who compensate for this weakness by gravitating instead to alternative perceptual targets, targets such as the non-biological world and its underlying principles of pattern, symmetry, repetition, structure and form?

Within the human population there are indeed individuals of this kind, and over the past century they have begun to be recognized. They are described most commonly as autistic.

Autism has given the scientific community a very difficult time. The condition was once regarded as extremely rare and almost always debilitating, but as evidence has accumulated over the years it has become more and more apparent that at least one percent of the human population can be accurately described as autistic, and along with such numbers has come the inevitable corollary that in the large majority of circumstances the condition cannot be all that debilitating. Autistic individuals certainly face some challenges, challenges that can vary in degree, but that has never prevented autistic individuals from blending in with the rest of the human population, so much so that they have gone virtually unrecognized for dozens of millennia. Nonetheless, even in the face of these undeniable facts, the scientific community has been unable to let go of its need to medicalize the condition, somehow convinced, without the slightest shred of evidence, that autism must be the result of biological defect. And so the research and studies have been growing like weeds—searches for defective genes, searches for defective neural pathways, searches for defective metabolisms— massively funded and massively peopled efforts that have now become laughable in the combined fruitlessness of their results. More troubling still, and certainly more shameful, has been the scientific community's willingness to heap insult and torment upon its autistic subjects, branding them with an assortment of inaccurate and unsupported labels (burdens, tragedies) and stifling them with an assortment of damaging treatments and so-called cures (applied behavioral analysis, stupefying drugs). The scientific community's current approach to autism is destined to become one of that community's more disgraceful hours.

The more informative approach to autism is to regard it as a condition of increased conspecific distance. The core characteristics of autism, what nearly every autistic individual shares in common, are the same characteristics predicted for an organism nearer to the conspecific boundary than the majority of its peers. Autistic individuals show less inclination for and less attention to their conspecific neighbors, a trait often presumed to be the evidence of damaged social functioning, but which is more precisely described as a diminished human awareness, an attenuated human recognition. Autistic children, less drawn to the activity of conspecific imitation, mature more slowly than do their non-autistic counterparts, sometimes taking well into adulthood to assume a fuller role within the broader population. Autistic individuals experience an assortment of sensory difficulties—hypersensitivity, hyposensitivity, synaesthesia—conditions with no discernible physical cause, meaning that these anomalies stem not from physical defect but instead from a generalized difficulty with the attainment of sensory unification. Finally, and almost invariably, autistic individuals compensate for their diminished conspecific awareness and recognition by focusing instead on alternative perceptual targets, including a predominance of targets from the non-biological world. In the youngest autistic individuals this characteristic is most often seen in the rapt attention given to such objects as spinning toys, symmetrical figures, repeating sounds and recurring scenes, while in older autistic individuals this tendency often coalesces into specialized and deeply learned interests. Misguidedly, the term *repetitive and restricted behaviors* is often used to disparage these concentrations on alternative perceptual targets, betraying a complete misunderstanding of both their essential purpose and their liberating consequence. For these concentrations on alternative perceptual targets are both the creative antidotes to what might otherwise be an overwhelming sensory chaos, and they are also the species' opening doors onto the organizing and intelligence-producing principles of pattern, symmetry, repetition, structure and form.

Autistics Perceive Differently

In their research paper *The Level and Nature of Autistic Intelligence II: What about Asperger Syndrome?*, Soulières et al. (2011) venture the following assertion:

> "Autistics [as compared to non-autistics] can maintain more veridical representations (e.g. representations closer to the actual information present in the environment) when performing high level, complex tasks."

That statement falls within the Soulières et al. tradition of depicting nearly every aspect of autistic perception as an *enhancement* or *advantage*, while offering little to no consideration for the notion that some aspects of autistic perception might constitute a relative *disadvantage*—the latter omission an inexplicable form of blindness. Nonetheless, the above statement cannot be dismissed, for by targeting veridical representation as the measuring stick for evaluating perceptual differences, Soulières et al. are tapping into a long-standing literature showing that autistic individuals perceive their world not only differently than do non-autistic individuals, but that autistic individuals perceive their world in a manner that under an unbiased perspective might be described as more objective or more factual. Of course *unbiased* is itself a charged word, and its application here must bear directly on the accuracy of the Soulières et al. assertion. And so it is worthwhile to give the above statement some further consideration—both to highlight the ways in which it is informative, and to highlight the ways in which it is mostly missing the point.

To investigate the Soulières et al. assertion regarding veridical representation, it will be useful to lay out a hypothetical visual scene (something similar could be done in the auditory domain if so desired). Once this visual scene has been fully described, it will then be necessary to consider how three different types of entities might survey this scene, including one entity intended to represent autistic perception and another entity intended to represent non-autistic perception. But as will become apparent shortly, when it comes to experiencing the more *veridical* representation of the visual scene, it is going to be the *third* entity that emerges as the clear winner in capturing "the actual information present in the environment."

Here is the scene: imagine a grassy field, similar to what one might come upon in a municipal park. Near the front of the field is a simple wooden bench where a woman and a young girl are seated and talking. Rising up behind them are four tall light poles, evenly spaced and situated so that they form a diagonal across the visual plane. The sky in the background is mostly blue with a few nondescript clouds straying past, and nothing else worthy of note is contained within the setting.

Here are three entities viewing this scene all from the exact same perspective, along with a rough description of what each perceives:

- Entity 1 surveys this scene entirely as a collection of light and color stimulus. One can think of this as a pixelated view, where the perception of this scene is best described as a set of points, each point determined by its relative position and by its light qualities, such as brightness and hue. Every feature within the scene is captured equally: the field, the bench, the people, the light poles, the sky—all are given exactly the same amount of observation and attention.

- Entity 2 surveys this scene and is immediately drawn to the woman and girl on the bench. If asked about this perception, Entity 2 might say something like, "Yes, I can see the mother and daughter sitting over there. See, the daughter is extremely upset—she's been crying." If asked about the light poles, Entity 2 might offer the observation that it is a good thing they have been installed here, because people can now come to the park at night without being afraid.

- Entity 3 surveys this scene and is struck by the particular arrangement of the light poles. Entity 3 might note that there are exactly four light poles, or might point out that they are evenly spaced, or might remark on the degree of angle they form across the visual plane. If asked about the people on the bench, Entity 3 might volunteer that they were noticed and there were exactly two of them and they looked small beneath the light poles towering above them.

Although each of these descriptions is intended to highlight only general tendencies, most people would agree that the perceptions of Entity 1 closely match those of a camera, that the perceptions of Entity 2 are fairly typical of a non-autistic person, and that the perceptions of Entity 3 are more indicative of someone who might be on the autism spectrum. Each entity *sees* the exact same visual stimulus, but each extracts from that stimulus an entirely different set of information—the essence of what is meant by the concept *perception*.

By most ways of thinking, Entity 1 has by far the most veridical representation here—Entity 1 comes the nearest to perceiving this visual scene as it truly is. The key to a camera creating an accurate visual representation is, ironically enough, not to do much of anything at all with it, in particular not to impose any kind of structure or filter upon the visual material. No foregrounding of information. No backgrounding of unneeded data. No extracting of signal from sensory noise. Just *reproduce* the visual scene as it actually is—that is all that a camera is expected or required to do.

By contrast, both Entity 2 and Entity 3 come to their particular perceptions by imposing some kind of structure or filter on the raw visual stimulus they receive—which is to say that some of the features in their visual field will emerge as perceptual foreground, while other features will fade almost entirely unobserved into the sensory background. The perceptual *process* is quite similar for both Entity 2 and Entity 3 (and quite different from the perceptual process of Entity 1), but what *distinguishes* the perceptions of Entity 2 and Entity 3 is the emergent material of the signal itself. That is to say, there is a categorical difference in what tends to foreground in the perceptions of Entity 2 versus what tends to foreground in the perceptions of Entity 3.

Note that nothing has been said so far that would make it obvious that Entity 3's representations are more veridical than those of Entity 2.

It is quite fortunate that Entity 1 is not a biological or responsive agent. If it were such an agent, having the most veridical representation of a visual scene would actually manifest as a huge liability. To be *responsive* to an environmental stimulus requires that information be extracted from it, exactly what Entity 1 is not designed to do. This has actually been a problem in the domain of robotics, where despite the availability of extremely accurate cameras, it has been nonetheless difficult to get machines to respond flexibly and constructively to various visual stimuli, precisely because it has been difficult to get machines to recognize what constitutes the essential foreground of a visual scene and what needs to be dismissed as inconsequential background. Possessing a perfectly veridical representation of an environmental stimulus is tantamount to experiencing sensory chaos; everything comes across as noise, nothing emerges as signal. And with no signal, there is no useful information, and with no useful information, there is no ability to respond with purpose.

This observation regarding the liability of a perfectly veridical representation is relevant to more than just the perceptual characteristics of Entity 1 (which after all, not being a biological agent, is not really vulnerable to the liability). As will be seen shortly, it is the *threat* of this liability that plays a critical role in the development of Entity 3's perceptual characteristics, characteristics that are motivated almost entirely by the need to avoid the debilitating sensory chaos that arises out of a perfectly veridical representation.

First, however, it is necessary to take a detour and consider further the perceptual characteristics of Entity 2 (non-autistic perception). By even the most casual observation, it is clear that the primary characteristic that delineates and defines non-autistic perception is its strong bias towards foregrounding *human* features within a sensory environment. Human faces, human voices, human movements, human actions. This is an instance of conspecific awareness and recognition, a trait common throughout the entire animal kingdom, whereby each organism is perceptually drawn primarily to the other members of its own species. In *Homo sapiens*, it is this human-specific perceptual focus that provides much of the necessary structuring and filtering that allows a person to extract meaningful and actionable signal from what would otherwise be sensory noise. The effects of this human-specific focus can be witnessed in the depiction of Entity 2's perception of the given visual scene, where attention is drawn first and foremost to the *people* within the scene, and in an impressively detailed manner. Even those features of the scene not directly connected to humankind are still brought to the foreground by an association to the species (the light poles for instance are comprehended as helping people see at night and not be afraid).

People-centric representations form much of the common thread that draws non-autistic cognition into a cohesive whole, and this common thread works on more than just an individual level. Since nearly every human *shares* this strong bias towards people-centric representations, these representations serve to coalesce not just individual thoughts and behaviors, but also the conventions and activities of the population as a whole. As is the case with nearly every other species upon this planet, the cohesion brought about by conspecific foregrounding delivers to humanity an entire array of biological and evolutionary benefits, directly supporting many survival and procreative efforts. And thus in a very real and observable way, non-autistic perception bestows to its possessors an essential and useful *advantage*, an advantage it would be folly to ignore.

The perceptions of Entity 3 (autistic perception) differ from those of its non-autistic counterpart precisely in the comparative lack of a human-specific focus. The difference is not absolute—autistic individuals to varying degree carry some level of natural attention for other people—but the difference is always large enough to produce significant effect, implying conspecific distance. The natural structuring and filtering of sensory experience provided by human faces, human voices, etc. is not strongly acquired in autistic individuals; for them, the coalescing impact of conspecific foregrounding goes mostly absent. As a result, autistic individuals find themselves in nearly the same circumstance as that of Entity 1, as that of a camera. Sensory impressions are received more raw and unfiltered, the details of the sensory field are processed more indiscriminately, and thus just as Soulières et al. would suggest, autistic perception approaches much nearer to that of veridical representation.

In this form, however, veridical representation does not offer any advantage or enhancement for autistic individuals; instead it manifests as a dangerous liability. Autistic individuals, quite unlike cameras, are biological agents, and to remain viable as biological agents they must be able to respond to their sensory environment with constructive purpose, they must be able to extract sensory signal and to ward off sensory noise.

Many of the developmental and sensory challenges that autistic individuals must endure and overcome can be traced to the inherent sensory chaos that accompanies a perfectly veridical representation, and to the extent that autistic individuals do achieve a level of advantage and enhancement from their condition, it is not because they come *nearer* to veridical representation but rather because they manage to *escape* it. Closed off from the coalescing benefit of conspecific perceptual foregrounding, autistic individuals must unify and organize their sensory experience by foregrounding instead an alternative target, and the target that autistic individuals almost invariably gravitate towards is the structural framework of the non-biological world. Pattern, number, repetition, symmetry: the same elements that break the background chaos of the non-biological world are the same elements appropriated by autistic individuals to help break the sensory chaos of their perceptual experience. This propensity to foreground the structural features of the surrounding environment is evident in the depiction of Entity 3's perception of the given visual scene, where attention is drawn first and foremost to the non-human artifacts, with an emphasis on the characteristics of pattern, symmetry, structure and form (the spacing and arrangement of the light poles for instance). Furthermore, in recalling how Entity 2 grasps the non-biological features of the visual scene by associating those features back to humanity, one can observe how Entity 3 effectively reverses this process, comprehending the *people* within the visual scene not by conspecific affinity, but instead by categorizing such people under structural characteristics, such as number and relative size.

In their pure form, autistic perception and non-autistic perception represent two different aspects of human perception that have now become so blended within the human population that in reality a pure version of either form is rarely encountered. Non-autistic perception stems from humanity's animal past and carries with it the strong and ancient influence of conspecific awareness and recognition, providing much of the binding that holds the species together and much of the vigor that drives the species to greater conquest. Autistic perception represents the atypical characteristics of humanity's recent perceptual turn, an unprecedented opening onto the world's structural and non-biological features, providing a means for overcoming many of the contingencies of survival and procreation, and providing the constructive vision for an exploration of a massively sized and massively detailed universe. Each form of perception offers an advantage the other cannot provide, and the strength of overall human perception has been its ability to combine the benefits of these two discordant constituents. For the species as a whole, the result of the combination of these two forms of perception has been astounding and prodigious, for quite unlike any other species—and quite unlike humans themselves from not that long ago—modern humans have been able to break the chains of biological constraint and are now rapidly building for themselves an environment of essentially unlimited potential.

To the extent that autistic perception flirts with the dangers of veridical representation, and to the extent that autistic perception ultimately draws its organization and unification from the structural features of the non-biological world, it is perhaps not unreasonable to suggest that autistic perception has something about it that can be described as more objective or more factual. But it is just as important to recognize that in its final form, autistic perception stands in *defiance* of veridical representation, and that in its structuring and filtering of environmental stimulus, autistic perception remains entirely analogous to its non-autistic counterpart. In truth, there is no unbiased perspective from which to judge the accuracy or advantage of differing forms of perception: each form of perception will be predisposed to favoring its own particular way of perceiving things. But when it comes to human perception, what matters is not the relative advantage or disadvantage of its constituent parts, what matters is the power of their amalgamation—the key to humanity having broken free of its former biological limitations, and the key to the world's structural framework having found a means to come to life.

Thus the lesson to be learned from autistic perception is simply this: autism is a perceptual *difference*, induced by the threat of a perceptual *liability*, resulting finally in a perceptual *enhancement* for the species as a whole.

Perception, Mathematics and Autism

Perception, including human perception, has not always been a consistently defined concept, but these days agreement can usually be reached somewhere along the following lines: animals receive, through their nervous system, a multitude of sensory impressions from which is distilled an awareness of the animal's environment, as well as a reaction back into that environment, and it is the *distillation* part of this process that stands at the core of what is typically called perception. Perception is necessary because the *entirety* of sensory experience would be too overwhelming. Unfiltered and undifferentiated sensory experience would produce only a chaotic awareness of the animal's environment, making enactment of targeted and productive reaction problematic at best. Perception extracts signal from sensory noise, perception distinguishes figure from sensory ground. It is the *foregrounded* elements of sensory experience that are precisely those elements that an animal perceives.

As such, particular *types* of perception can be defined in large measure by highlighting the characteristics of what tends to foreground within that type of perception, and by juxtaposing those characteristics against what remains ignored or unperceived. Applying this technique across the entire animal kingdom is instructive, for it reveals a broadly consistent and unifying theme. As any regular observer of nature shows could easily attest, the attentive focus of wild animals is highly predictable and generally unvaried across the many species, and can be classified under just a small set of headings: food, water, danger, shelter, family, sexual targets, sexual rivals, predators, prey, conspecifics. There is of course nothing random or surprising in that list, each of its components plays a critical role in the struggle for survival and procreation; this type of perception is universal precisely because it serves the biological process. Nonetheless, while noting these characteristics of what tends to foreground within animal perception, it is also instructive to consider those sensory features that go undiscerned. The wind rustling in the grass and leaves. Wisps of cloud drifting overhead. An arrangement of bushes along the distant horizon. Unless such features happen to play a direct role in an animal's quest for survival and procreation, they will go almost entirely unnoticed, and this will be true of a very large portion of an animal's sensory experience—it will simply fade unobserved into the sensory background.

It would be useful to give a name to this universal predisposition to foreground primarily, if not exclusively, those sensory features that are essential to survival and procreation. This predisposition can be labeled *biological perception*. And as a supplement, it would be useful also to give a categorizing name to the foregrounded sensory features themselves (that is to say, food, sexual rivals, predators, etc.). This category can be called *darwinamatics*—an awkward sounding name to be sure, but one chosen because it corresponds nicely to its ready-made counterpart, a counterpart that will be considered shortly.

Human perception is intriguing because it is both animal perception and it is not: like animal perception, human perception adheres to biological perception's rule of universality, and yet unlike animal perception, human perception provides the only known counterexample to biological perception's rule of exclusivity.

That human perception *is* a form of biological perception can be seen readily enough from two distinct considerations. First, there is anthropological history, which reveals that for an extremely long period of time after the evolutionary split from the other apes, human existence— and along with it, human perception—must have remained as animal-like as for all the other beasts. From *Australopithecus* down through the later species *Homo*, there is little in the way of evidence to suggest that mankind's foregrounded focus and endeavor ever deviated far from the immediate constraints and concerns of survival and procreation. Some would argue that this perceptual state of affairs must have remained constant until as recently as around fifty thousand years ago, but at whatever moment one places the timing of mankind's perceptual turn, it is certain that the human species possessed nothing more than a strictly biological perception for a very long period of time.

The second consideration demonstrating that human perception is a form of biological perception can be observed directly today. For although modern human perception can no longer be defined strictly in terms of biological perception alone, modern human perception still retains the vast majority of its former biological traits. In observing the features that tend to foreground within human awareness, one recognizes that food, sex, danger and all the rest continue to play an extremely prominent role—that is to say, darwinamatics still constitutes much of the focus of human attention and endeavor. Indeed a healthy dose of biological perception is considered to be crucial for both early development and everyday functioning, with those judged to be inadequately attuned to such things as family, rivalries and conspecifics judged also to be the bearers of various psychological or developmental disorders. The foregrounded elements associated with survival and procreation may no longer play the critical role they once did on the prehistoric savanna, but they still motivate and drive much of the action in a modern human society.

Thus biological perception is not the characteristic that distinguishes human perception from animal perception—that characteristic is still shared in common. What distinguishes human perception from animal perception is that human perception, and human perception alone, has acquired a significant addendum. In the foreground of modern human awareness, in addition to the still influential components associated with survival and procreation, one finds also an entire host of sights, sounds and other sensory features that no wild animal would ever naturally discern. A list of such features would stretch to enormous length, and it would include not only the symbols of language, the architectural traits of buildings, the rhythms of music and the intoxications of perfume, it would include also the wind rustling in the grass and leaves, wisps of cloud drifting overhead, and an arrangement of bushes along the distant horizon. Modern man now foregrounds a vast range of sensory features not directly connected to the immediate concerns of survival and procreation, which is to say that modern man has acquired a second and entirely different type of perception.

This second type of perception is distinguished primarily by its gravitation towards non-biological targets and by its persistent foregrounding of structural characteristics, characteristics that can be classified under just a small set of headings—symmetry, pattern, mapping, order, form. The same structural principles that unify and organize the objective world now increasingly unify and organize human sensory experience. Furthermore, humans have been making prolific use of these newfound principles to reconstruct their surrounding environment, forging an increasingly receptive home for this new type of perception, nudging the distinctiveness of the present age towards a *constructed* distinctiveness, in fierce defiance of nature and its biologically limiting constraints. Humans have become as proficient with the *artificial* as they once were with the *natural,* and the human population is now foregrounding a veritable cornucopia of number, shape, order, rule. Thus quite unlike any other species on this planet—and quite unlike humans themselves of not that long ago—modern humans find themselves focusing on an entirely different type of sensory target, a target not strictly associated with survival and procreation, a target capable of producing radical influence and astounding effect.

As was done with the phrase *biological perception,* it would be useful to give a name to this exclusively human capacity to foreground those sensory features that possess structural and patterned characteristics. This capacity can be labeled *logical perception.* And again, as was done with the term *darwinamatics,* it would be useful to give a categorizing name to the foregrounded sensory features themselves (that is to say, symmetry, order, mapping, etc.). This time, however, there is no need to invent a term, for there is one already in widespread and common use. That term is *mathematics.* The study of symmetry, order, mapping, etc. is none other than the study of mathematics.

Thus to summarize, modern human perception consists fundamentally of a blend of two very different types of perception. The first type of perception foregrounds those sensory features directly associated with survival and procreation. This type of perception has been labeled *biological perception,* and its foregrounded sensory features have been categorized as *darwinamatics.* It is recognized that humans share this type of perception with all the other animals, have inherited it from out of the species' animal past, and continue to experience its influence within the modern age. The second type of perception, unique to humans and acquired quite recently within anthropological history, foregrounds those sensory features that make up the structural framework of the non-biological world and that possess the underlying characteristics of pattern, symmetry, structure and form. This second type of perception has been labeled *logical perception,* and it has been recognized that the foregrounded sensory characteristics of logical perception are precisely those characteristics commonly studied under the heading of *mathematics*.

Mathematics has always been something of a philosophical puzzle. Intimately connected to space and time and the underpinning behind almost every facet of rational thought, mathematics appears to stand at the core of all non-biological conception, and so it has been more than a little bit tantalizing to try to determine the foundations of mathematics itself. The ancient Greeks were already arguing the matter fiercely, including Plato and his idealized forms, and in more recent times such esteemed thinkers as Leibniz and Kant have made widely influential and sometimes controversial contributions. The twentieth century saw the rise and battle of three competing schools of thought—the logicist, formalist and intuitionist points of view—and at various times and in various ways, the ultimate source of mathematics has been attributed in turn to God, human intuition, the external world, and the neural mechanisms inside the human skull (the latter being perhaps the most mythical suggestion of them all). Yet despite all these competing proposals—or perhaps *because* of all these competing proposals—the philosophical puzzle has remained as puzzling as ever.

But here is a proposal: the above-stated recognition of mathematics as being the equivalent of the foregrounded elements within humanity's second type of perception can open the door to a less mythical and more directly observable explanation for the origin and foundation of mathematics. The similarities between logical perception and biological perception already begin to point the way, for there has never been any philosophical qualms regarding the origin and foundation of darwinamatics—the targets of biological perception have always been approached as simply open to inspection, and there is no reason to think that the targets of logical perception cannot be approached in precisely the same way. Plus the placement of logical perception's birth within the recent time frame of human history provides still more reason to conceive of mathematics as being something other than mystical—instead history suggests that mathematics can be more soberly described as simply the outcome of an anthropological event, as simply the outcome of the advent of logical perception.

Of course if that is all that were being offered, one might reasonably complain that this "sober" description of mathematics does little more than change the aspect of the problem, it makes out of logical perception the same philosophical puzzle that was previously being made of mathematics itself. What would be the origin and foundation of logical perception? Would it be a gift from the gods? how about an irreducible human intuition? or perhaps an evolutionary explosion of synaptic generation? As it turns out, in the early twenty-first century humans have been slowly uncovering a patch of knowledge that has the ability to make it clear that the origin and foundation of logical perception is in fact none of the above. Instead logical perception can be seen as directly attributable—and in a directly observable way—to the presence and influence of an atypical group of people.

Autism, a distinctive set of biological, sensory and developmental characteristics, is usually labeled as a medical condition, but at its root, autism is more accurately and more insightfully described as a condition defined by perception. Indeed in many respects, what distinguishes autism and non-autism—each condition regarded in its purest form—is exactly the same distinction to be made between logical perception and biological perception. Because what determines and unifies autistic experience is its diminished bias towards biological perception, and in particular its diminished foregrounding of conspecifics. Most individuals, strongly under the influence of the species' ongoing attachment to biological perception, easily foreground and attend to the other members of the human population. But autistic individuals, to varying degree *detached* from the influence of biological perception, find themselves with little perceptual affinity for the other humans around them. Autistic individuals do not readily foreground human voices, they do not focus energetically on human faces, they do not enthrall to the most common human concerns. This diminished awareness towards the other members of the species is observable from a very early age in autistic individuals and it remains extremely consistent—to the point of being defining—across the entirety of the autistic population. This diminished awareness towards the other members of the species is compensated for only slowly and with great effort throughout an elongated developmental process, and it continues to produce many subtle social anomalies well into advanced age. Whereas the common animal experience is to foreground first and foremost those sensory features connected with a species' survival and procreation—including a strong proclivity towards the perceptual foregrounding of conspecifics—autistic individuals now serve as the only known counterexample to this otherwise universal tendency, and thus autistic individuals can be described as the least animal-like of

Earth's many biological creatures, because autistic individuals are the least determined by the characteristics and constraints of biological perception.

As a result of their diminished facility with biological perception autistic individuals are initially hindered in gaining their sensory footing—for them, little can emerge as sensory signal, there is almost no figure against the sensory ground. If this set of sensory circumstances were to continue to hold, then autistic individuals would find themselves in the most dire of straits, possessing almost no sensory traction to aid in their developmental progress or in their tackling of the essential requirements of survival itself. Fortunately, this set of sensory circumstances generally does not hold. In the absence of a strong type of perception—that is to say, in the absence of biological perception—autistic individuals find themselves with both the opportunity and the motivation to latch onto *alternative* types of perception, and the alternative type of perception that emerges the most prominently for autistic individuals is the type of perception described above as logical perception. It is those same sensory features that embody symmetry, pattern, mapping, structure and form that are the sensory features most capable of breaking a background sensory chaos, and thus autistic individuals, hungry for perceptual targets that can make order out of their otherwise chaotic sensory world, gravitate to these alternative perceptual targets with an almost fanatical intensity. Lining up toys, preoccupation with spinning objects, repetitive flapping of hands, extreme iteration over video and song, idiosyncratic dexterity with letters and numbers—these characteristic behaviors, observable from the earliest age in autistic children, betray a deep fascination with sensory targets composed out of pattern, structure and form. Instead of the common perceptual bias towards other humans and their species-driven endeavors, autistic individuals find themselves drawn to number, shape, order, rule. Instead of a natural ease with the material of darwinamatics, autistic individuals gravitate almost obsessively to the world of mathematics.

(All this is observable. It is to the great shame of modern science that in its insistence on medicalizing autism, and in its pursuit of so many mercenary distractions—including an endless, self-serving touting of treatment, intervention and cure—modern science has failed to make these observations itself. It remains unclear when science will begin to make its *own* perceptual turn, but at the moment the prognosis remains highly pessimistic.)

The history of mathematics provides still more evidence of a direct connection between mathematical and autistic characteristics. Although the biographical details are not always complete and although nearly every famed mathematician lived well before the recognition of autism, even one glance at the lives of Archimedes, Gauss, Newton, Euler, Riemann, Lagrange, Cantor, Fermat, Gödel and Turing will make it obvious that autism must have been lingering somewhere near at hand. There is not one social butterfly among these men, not one glad-handing denizen of the weekly cocktail party, and one can assume it must have been so even at the very beginning, when shape and number were first espied. Mathematics is a strange and lonely pursuit, a calling more tantalizing to those unattached to the immediate concerns of everyday society and more compelled by the patterned arrangements of the external world. Those who are biased towards biological perception will tend to become merchants, managers and politicians; those who are biased towards logical perception will tend to become physicists, programmers and engineers; and those who are perceptually obsessed by the basic elements of pattern, symmetry, structure and form will become the prime candidates to serve as mathematicians. Everyone is drawn to the path he or she most clearly perceives.

A not unreasonable conjecture would be to say that logical perception first made its appearance on this planet starting around fifty thousand years ago, when autistic individuals first began to achieve significant presence and influence within the human population (rising to the one to two percent level of prevalence that can be measured today). Employing their structure-grounded proclivities to reconstruct various aspects of their environment—and thereby helping to introduce the features of language, art and number into the human surroundings—autistic individuals would have begun to pave the way to logical perception for the entire human population, leveraging the natural inclination of most humans to do what other humans do. In turn, the non-autistic population would have maintained the connection to the biological concerns and ambitions of species, helping to thrust both populations forward in an expansive and explosive conquest of survival and procreation. In today's prodigiously human world, each individual now enjoys the benefit of this dual influence, with pure forms of either logical perception or biological perception, as well as the correspondingly pure forms of autism or non-autism, now exceptionally rare (and most often with challenging consequence). In the modern world, while continuing to display the outward behavioral signs of one's more natural inclination, each individual learns to employ a blended form of both logical perception and biological perception.

Thus to summarize once more, it has been recognized that mathematics is the general term to be applied to the foregrounded sensory features that arise within logical perception, and it has also been recognized that the origin of logical perception can be traced to the atypical perceptual characteristics of the autistic population. This latter recognition places the subject of mathematics into a more natural context, it allows one to confidently forgo such unobservable notions of mathematics as being for instance the mind of God, the fruit of human intuition, the cold formality of the external world, or the magical product of neural modules inside the human head. Instead, mathematics can be described more directly and more openly as being the natural consequence of the presence and influence of autistic individuals within the human population, the natural consequence of their readily observable, albeit highly unusual form of perception. Thus mathematics can be grounded as an anthropological fact.

Recognizing mathematics to be an anthropological fact—a fact of perception—has consequences for the *practice* of mathematics. Throughout its historical development, mathematics has frequently become entangled in controversies of legitimacy, controversies spawned by questions not of calculation or deduction but questions over whether certain proposed concepts can be considered genuinely mathematical. Here too the ancient Greeks already were well engaged, wrestling with the status of irrational numbers and with the validity of actual (completed) infinities. In more recent years, disputes have arisen regarding infinitesimals, the cardinal number of sets, and existence proofs that rely upon the law of excluded middle. These matters are easily argued but not so easily resolved, and thus opposing camps are apt to form and the debates to run on and on. The dilemma here is that if mathematics itself is not well grounded, then there are no practical means for settling questions of legitimacy. When the ultimate arbiter is taken to be God, intuition or perhaps a mass of neurons, the combatants are free to shift the foundation to fit their own particular case.

Thus the key to finding pragmatic means to help resolve mathematical legitimacy disputes is to develop some grounding for mathematics itself, and the key to developing some grounding for mathematics is to recognize the critical role being played by perception. The proposal being made here is that nearly every mathematical legitimacy concern comes down ultimately to a question of perception—and in particular, comes down to a question of *foregrounding* within perception. Always at the moment of dispute, always at the point of crossover from general agreement to widespread debate, there can be found a mathematical concept struggling to achieve its perceptual grounds.

Take the case of an actual (completed) infinity. By and large, modern humans have little difficulty or disagreement about foregrounding a finite sequence (one, two, three, four); they sense the distinctiveness of this perception as surely as they trust their ability to construct the sequence's numbers within the terrain of their physical environment. Furthermore, in addition to the constructed sequence itself, humans can foreground quite easily each step of the iterative sequential process (take something, add one to get its successor, take the successor, add one to get the successor of the successor, and so on). This recipe is sharply defined and open to assessment by the senses, and thus no dispute or uncertainty ever arises about its nature.

But with an infinite sequence, something becomes different—perceptually different. The iterative sequential process remains entirely unobjectionable, because it remains essentially the same: each step in the process is still as prominent and surveyable as all the previous steps, with the fact that the steps now come to no end being seen as inconsequential to their perceptual foregrounding. But the *completed* sequence is another matter. A fully realized infinite set is precisely the thing that does not foreground within human perception, and it remains doubtful whether finite phrases such as "actual infinity" or "infinite set"—or axioms attached to such phrases—can alleviate the uncertainty. Many humans are unsatisfied with symbols or axioms that serve as *substitutes* for perceptual foregrounding, especially when what those symbols or axioms *represent* remain hidden as noise within the perceptual field. The ancient Greeks, as well as more recent mathematicians such as Gauss, have readily dismissed the notion of an actual infinity, while many other mathematicians have firmly disagreed.

As another example, the irrational numbers have long produced a sense of queasiness among mathematicians, and the introduction of techniques such as the *Dedekind cut* were motivated precisely by the need to place the irrational numbers on much firmer ground. And yet when it comes to the firmer ground associated with logical human perception, much of the queasiness still remains. Dedekind cuts define the real numbers via unique divisions of the rational numbers into two order-based sets—for instance a Left set of rational numbers that are less than or equal to the given number and a Right set of rational numbers that are strictly greater than the given number. Proponents of the technique can then provide many examples that demonstrate how such cuts distinctly determine particular irrational numbers—the square root of 2, the arctangent of 3, the natural logarithm of 5. Although doubts may linger about the use of completed infinities to form these Left and Right sets, for anyone who has ever followed the mechanics of an actual Dedekind cut, it is hard not to be impressed by the vividness of the technique. In the examples typically offered, the process of a Dedekind cut gives the appearance, by and large, of a technique with strong perceptual grounds.

Unfortunately, perceptually speaking, the examples typically offered are not the instances most in question. Long before a Dedekind cut was ever considered, various mathematical techniques had been developed to foreground particular types of irrational numbers—including for instance the square root of 2, the arctangent of 3, and the natural logarithm of 5. Indeed in many cases it is precisely the existence of such techniques that makes an actualized Dedekind cut conceivable in the usual sense, and so for those humans who are convinced only by the evidence firmly linked to their own perception, a Dedekind cut arrives as little more than the proverbial white elephant. In those cases of irrational numbers that can already be perceptually foregrounded through an alternative technique, a Dedekind cut comes across as ostentatiously superfluous; and in those cases of irrational numbers that possess no conceivable foregrounding technique, the Dedekind cut proves to be little better than useless. Nonetheless, there are many mathematicians who would strenuously argue otherwise.

Finally, one might consider the circumstances surrounding the concept of negation and the arguments *reductio ad absurdum* based upon negation. A sense of the controversy can be highlighted with just a rough sketch:

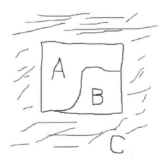

In this image, there is a square region that foregrounds perceptually, and within that square region there are two clearly demarcated sub-regions (A and B). Outside the square region there is an unbounded region that has been labeled C, and this unbounded region is intended to depict whatever has not been otherwise described—a phrase intended to be precisely vague. Perceptually speaking, negation within the context of the square is unproblematic, because every region and sub-region foregrounds quite easily. For instance, within the context of the square, the negation of A is the region B and the negation of B is the region A, and neither of these negations is perceptually troubling. But negation in the context of the *entire picture* is perceptually more ambiguous. For instance, the negation of the square region itself (that is, the negation of A union B) comes across much differently than in the former case: the square region still foregrounds quite easily, but the negation of the square region does not—in fact, the best that might be said of the region C is that it does an admirable job of forming the background chaos. When mathematicians treat these two instances of negation as similar or equivalent, it is not surprising that disputes can quickly follow. And in a similar manner, lurking behind almost every instance of an argument over an existence proof relying upon the law of excluded middle, one can find a similar instance of perceptual ambiguity, a piece of the mathematical landscape struggling to be clearly seen.

It is not the intention of this essay to adjudicate these matters. The purpose behind these examples is to demonstrate that mathematical legitimacy disputes are still quite common and go generally unresolved, and this because mathematics itself has remained largely ungrounded. But with what has been said regarding perception—biological, logical and autistic—and with an understanding that mathematics has grown organically out of human circumstances, there is an opportunity to examine mathematics with a more anthropological eye. Armed with an awareness of the history behind logical and autistic perception, and recognizing that issues of perceptual foregrounding lurk behind nearly every known mathematical dispute, one can begin to approach these disputes from an entirely different direction, one more on par with efforts taken towards biological perception and darwinamatics. Thus it is no longer appropriate to make mathematical appeals to such concepts as divinity, intuition or specialized neurons. Humans will be much better served by grounding their mathematics in history, in anthropology, in the details—the *perceptual* details—of their everyday lives. Humans will begin to make progress on questions of mathematical legitimacy when they begin to place their mathematical concepts on the same perceptual footing as they would a sexual encounter, a live birth, or a tasty meal.

This short essay has offered a fresh journey through the world of mathematics. The journey began with the topic of perception and with the recognition that in addition to the animal-inherited characteristics of biological perception, humanity has recently in its anthropological history acquired a second type of perception, logical perception, in which the foregrounded sensory features are precisely those features that belong to the category of mathematics. Next, the behaviors and inclinations of autistic individuals have been explored with an unprejudiced eye, giving particular focus to the atypical characteristics of autistic sensory attention, leading ultimately to the conclusion that logical perception must have arisen directly from autistic perception, and that it has been the presence and influence of the autistic population that has served as the catalyst for bringing logical perception and mathematics into the human world. Finally, it has been ventured that the establishment of mathematics as an anthropological fact has provided means for reassessing many mathematical disputes, means that are more practical and more informative than resorting to myth, intuition or unexplained neural magic.

Genius

There is a widespread misconception, common among laypeople and many academicians too, that genius is the equivalent of greater intelligence. This can be seen for instance in the tendency to categorize high IQ scores, such as those above 150, as falling within a genius range, and reciprocally it can be seen in the anachronistic practice of doling out impressive IQ scores— usually in the neighborhood of 200 or so—to well-established geniuses such as Mozart and Newton. To be fair, many researchers do recognize that the possession of a high IQ is not sufficient to establish genius, that other factors must also be brought to bear. For instance creativity frequently gets mentioned as a necessary concomitant to genius, and others have noted the tendency towards aloofness and oddity that many geniuses seem to exude. Still for most people, it is hard not to conceive of a direct relationship between genius and greater intelligence, in many respects the relationship seems so blatantly obvious. And this remains so even though such a relationship would these days give rise to a troubling conundrum: in this era of the Flynn effect, when intelligence is everywhere measurably on the rise, it has to be downright puzzling as to why genius is not blossoming around every corner, indeed why it seems to have almost entirely disappeared.

The irony here is that there *is* a direct relationship between genius and greater intelligence—the blatantly obvious turns out in this case to be actually true—and yet this direct relationship remains entirely misapprehended. The trouble lies perhaps not so much with the concept of genius itself, a concept that remains fluid enough to still be amended. The trouble lies more fundamentally with the concept of intelligence, a concept that has now hardened into intransigent dogma. Humanity thoroughly misunderstands what intelligence is, and thus in turn, it thoroughly misunderstands what genius is.

Perhaps no statement is in less dispute than the following: intelligence is a neural activity, it is what humans produce inside their evolutionarily superior brain. Indeed when humans applaud a high IQ score (and in the same breath applaud genius), what they believe they are paying homage to is the activities of someone's brain, they are giving their due to a presumed instance of neural excellence. People's brains are *wired* to be smart, it seems that everyone knows that by now, and if a person has managed to improve his intelligence through education or some other means, it is because he has managed to rearrange the intricate workings inside his skull, he has had recourse to that marvelous (and practically miraculous) concept known as neural plasticity. As a weightlifter can harvest the strength of his over-sized muscles, an ingenious thinker can brandish the power of his super-connected neurons: such notions have become the unquestioned dogma of the land.

As with many other well-entrenched dogmatic mistakes, this one began honestly enough with a grain of truth. That there are natural intelligence differences from person to person would have been apparent even before the dawn of civilization, and now with the advent of intelligence exams and psychometric analysis, these distinctions have not only been experimentally confirmed, they have been broadly linked to genetic and neurological foundations. So the brain certainly does play an important role in human intelligence, of that there can be no doubt. But that the brain plays the *entire* role in human intelligence, or even the most *significant* role, that is something that might have been doubted from the very beginning.

The primary indicator that intelligence cannot be explained by human neurology alone is the Flynn effect, the observation that intelligence scores have been increasing population wide since first being measured. If intelligence is indeed exclusively a brain-based activity, then the Flynn effect implies that human neurology must be rapidly and tangibly changing, becoming substantively more effective with each generation. Scientists hesitate before such a notion, because it defies every known characteristic of physiology, genetics and evolution—populations do not change that dramatically from generation to generation, such an occurrence would be biologically unprecedented. Therefore scientists look to alternative explanations to justify the Flynn effect, a grand plethora of alternative explanations—heterosis, better nutrition, social multipliers, video games, increased schooling, test familiarity, fast and slow life. But despite these many suggestions, the Flynn effect remains essentially unexplained, and the unavoidable consequence seems to be this: the Flynn effect is incompatible with an entirely neurological human intelligence, meaning that ultimately one of those two concepts must go. And the Flynn effect is an observation, while an entirely neurological human intelligence is merely an assumption.

Plus it is more than just the Flynn effect that speaks against this notion of a brain-based intelligence. Genius too seems to be utterly incompatible with the concept. Because if intelligence really were exclusively a brain-produced activity, then the common wisdom regarding genius would precisely thereby become true. Genius would be the product of the more effective neural structures, and in this era of an ever-increasing intelligence, genius will have become as plentiful as springtime rain. But genius is not more common in the modern era, it remains as rare today as it ever was, the population's greater intelligence notwithstanding. Thus the unavoidable consequence seems to be this: the characteristics of genius simply do not fit to the characteristics of an entirely neurological human intelligence, meaning that ultimately one of those two concepts must go. And the characteristics of genius are derived from observation, while an entirely neurological human intelligence is merely an assumption.

In the essay *The Flynn Effect's Unseen Hand* a description of intelligence is detailed that rejects primary reliance upon an exclusively neurological foundation. In this new description, intelligence is defined more directly as being the amount of pattern, structure and form tangibly contained within the human environment. The network of highways, the symmetry of buildings, the repetition of clocks, the arrangement of letters upon a page, these many artificial environmental features constitute the material substance of intelligence itself—directly observable, directly measurable, directly defined. Intelligence palpably exists *around* a human, it does not exist primarily inside his head. And although humans differ in their ability to absorb and respond to this surrounding intelligence, a difference with genetic and neural basis, the *overall* level of human intelligence is not determined by the sum of individual neural abilities, the overall level of human intelligence is not the combined product of many human brains. Instead intelligence grows via the concrete addition of pattern, structure and form into the human environment, and it is this physical accretion of environmental intelligence that constitutes the direct source, the direct driver and the direct cause of the Flynn effect.

Plus this new description of intelligence does more than provide an accounting of the Flynn effect, it also leads to a straightforward and observable definition of genius. Accumulation of intelligence into the human environment does not happen by way of magic; in order for new intelligence to accrue within the human surroundings something must put it there. A large portion of this accumulation can be accomplished via replication, by copying the already existent pattern, structure and form from one context into another. Blueprints, books, education, communication, plus a myriad of other means—all these devices serve to take the intelligence already embodied within the human environment and then spread it further around. But replication can only go so far. If intelligence is to continue to grow, then *novel* pattern, structure and form must eventually be introduced. And while replication can be achieved by almost anyone (it is humanity's greatest shared activity), the introduction of novel intelligence is an activity reserved for the very few. What is needed for this unusual feat is an individual with an exceptionally unusual eye, an individual with both the ability and inclination to perceive the world not as it already is and not as others already perceive it, but to perceive the world quite differently from everyone else, to cast the world into a whole new paradigm. And only after these anomalous perceptions have been promulgated far enough, only after they have been copied a sufficient enough times, only after they have significantly increased the overall amount of pattern, structure and form contained within the human environment, only then can the source of these catalyzing perceptions be finally recognized, often very much in retrospect, and the originating individual can be given the name he or she most accurately deserves, can be given the name of genius.

Genius is the fountainhead of increasing intelligence within the human environment, it is not the result of greater intelligence inside the human head. In short, genius is the spark that fires the Flynn effect.

The telltale characteristic of genius is its deep fascination with non-biological pattern, structure and form, the material substance of intelligence itself. It is a fascination that can often border on the aberrant. This characteristic already establishes the rarity of genius, because for most humans their primary focus is not on non-biological pattern, structure and form, for most humans their primary focus is on other people. This is in keeping with the powerful hold that biological perception and conspecific awareness have upon nearly every animal organism, a hold essential to survival and procreation but a hold effectively blinding to the possibilities of new intelligence. The individual genius is one who has been mostly *loosened* from this conspecific grip and who in compensation has turned hungrily towards the structural details of the surrounding world. This perceptual mismatch between the individual genius and the remainder of humanity explains in large measure the oft-mentioned secondary traits of genius: iconoclastic, abrasive, aloof, strange. The individual genius simply does not perceive the world as does everyone else—genius and humanity are fundamentally at odds.

The characteristics of genius align closely to the characteristics of the condition known as autism. In each case, these are individuals conspecifically distanced from the remainder of the population. In each case, these are individuals focused primarily on non-biological pattern, structure and form (and not focused primarily on other people). In each case, these are individuals misunderstood and frequently disdained by conventional wisdom. To those who have callously written off the autistic population, including nearly the entire scientific community, this alignment of genius and autism will seem nothing short of outrageous. But the observable characteristics of genius and autism speak eloquently for themselves, characteristics that align with typicality hardly at all.

The acclaim that typically attaches to genius is perhaps its most ironic feature, in part because each occasion of genius is celebrated as though it could not have been otherwise, as though its originator were neurally predestined for the momentous task. But in fact, in a context of accruing intelligence, nearly every instance of genius involves a discovery that was destined to be made sooner or later anyway. Take Newton for instance: if Newton had not returned home in his twenty-third year but instead had traveled to London and therein succumbed to the Great Plague, it does not mean that the differential calculus, the laws of motion and the theory of gravitation would have never seen the light of day. Other individuals of eccentric perception would have eventually discovered and promoted these notions, and today those individuals would be heralded as genius. As far as is known, there may have been several predecessors to Newton all capable of his exact same feats, but who through unfortunate circumstance never gained the opportunity.

The more authentic reason to celebrate genius is that it is an act of individual defiance and individual courage. The approbation often showered upon genius is always done so from the safety of retrospective time, after the favorable consequences of the ingenious act have had adequate years to become well established. But at the moment of its birth, novel intelligence will always cut against the common grain and thus will gather no immediate stamp of approval. Instead, what novel intelligence usually gathers is neglect, scorn and derision. Humanity is content with what it already knows, it feels the bravest with what it can perceive in unison—and thus each revision is greeted as a hostile intruder. To bring pristine pattern, structure and form into the human environment, the individual genius will discover he must weather a storm of rebukes from without and a flood of doubts from within—the introduction of new intelligence is one of the loneliest acts imaginable.

This past century has seen a grand-scale movement to accommodate genius to a broader population. Perhaps motivated by genius's retrospective acclaim, and likely unaware of the requisite isolation, humanity has been pooling its efforts in an attempt to distill genius's indispensable merits into dispensable recipe. Scientific method and artistic technique have emerged as the templates of choice, and the academic institutions, once home to the most bizarre and misanthropic of creatures, today attract gregarious millions, each eager to play a role in the next great discovery. Optimism is announced daily by press release, pending results form the backbone of nearly every grant proposal, but there is an awkward silence now surrounding the din of these swelling universities. It is the silence of genius having walked away from these overcrowded academic halls.

The ever-more tightly prescribed requirements of scientific method have been leading to an all-too-predictable result, a tidal-wave of bland minutiae, more monotonous and more dogmatic with each publication. The increasingly rote specifications of artistic technique have been leading to a similarly predictable result, an avalanche of trivial art for trivial art's sake, more self-conscious and more self-congratulatory with each debut. Having pooled their efforts in the hopes of being part of something cognitively grand, today's university denizens find themselves herded along in an increasingly frantic race for more: more requirements, more specifications, more standards, more ethics, more committees, more peers, more reviews, more co-authors, more citations, more statistics, more funding. The promise seems to be that if everyone would just stick together, if everyone would just follow the routine, then the fruits of genius could flow forth like manna and honey, could flow forth as the combined product of everyone's evolutionarily superior brain. And thus the grand-scale movement has morphed into a music-hall comedy, full of bathos and farce.

Genius does not work this way. Genius attaches to individuals, it does not arise from groups. Indeed genius appears only in those who have mastered that rarest characteristic of all—the willingness to dare to go it alone. Although scientific method and artistic technique will always have their place, as tools in the massive *replication* of intelligence, still the honorable work of all mankind, nonetheless, scientific method and artistic technique have no power to inspire genius. And as the academic institutions become increasingly shoulder to shoulder, as they sink further into a slavedom of prescribed routine, it can be expected that the individual genius will continue to hasten away. It can be expected that the next great discovery will come from someplace unexpected.

Bibliography

Dickens, W. T. & Flynn, J. R. (2001). Heritability estimates versus large environmental effects: The IQ paradox resolved. *Psychological Review*, 108: 346–369.

Flynn, J. R. (1999). Searching for justice: The discovery of IQ gains over time. *American Psychologist, 54,* 5–20.

Flynn, J. R. (2007). *What is intelligence? Beyond the Flynn effect.* New York: Cambridge University Press.

Greenfield, P. (1998). The cultural evolution of IQ. In U. Neisser (Ed.), *The rising curve.* Washington, DC: American Psychological Association.

Lewontin, R. C. (1976). Further remarks on race and the genetics of intelligence; Race and intelligence. In N. J. Block & G. Dworkin (eds.), *The IQ controversy.* New York: Pantheon Books.

Schooler, C. (1998). Environmental complexity and the Flynn effect. In U. Neisser (Ed.), *The rising curve.* Washington, DC: American Psychological Association.

Soulières I., Dawson M., Gernsbacher M. A., Mottron L. (2011) The Level and Nature of Autistic Intelligence II: What about Asperger Syndrome? *PLoS ONE 6(9): e25372.* doi:10.1371/journal.pone.0025372

Printed in the United States
By Bookmasters